MODERN PSYCHIATRY

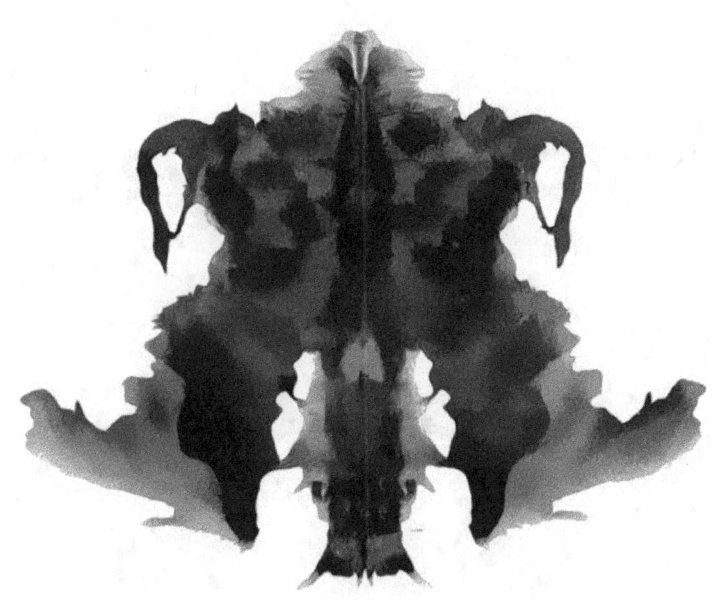

AN THIRD MILLENIUM VIEWING

Psychoanalyzes New School

INDEX

INTRO

PSYCHIATRIC MORDEN VIEWING ....

"HISTORICAL CONTEX"

ECONOMIC STRUNGGLE.......................................

VIOLENCE CARENESS......................................

TRUMPISMUS.......................................

"PSYCHOANALIZES 21 CENTURYES"

SYSTEM PRISION.......................................

TRANSFERENCE.......................................

PSYCHOANALIZES FROM NEO CONTEMPORARY
WORLD.......................................

SOCIAL INFERIORITY COMPLEX...

PARANOIDISMUS UNTRUETH...

TWO KIDS AUTISMUS AMONG...

PSYCHOANALIZES ESSAY.......................................

BAD DIAGNOSIS.......................................

APOOR ESSAY OTHER ESSAY.......................................

EUDIPHICAL COMPLEX ESSAY PART ONE...

ONE SOCIAL PERSONALITY.......................................

PARANOIDISMUS UNTRUETH.......................................

BARRIER SUICIDE.......................................

WRONG THERAPY..

EUDIPHICAL COMPLEX ESSAY PART TWO..

EUDIPHICAL COMPLEX ESSAY PART THREE..

EUDIPHICAL COMPLEX ESSAY PART FOUR..

SOCIAL SPLINTER STILL PERSONALITY..

INTRO

PSYCHIATRIC'S MODERN VIEWING

In postcontemporary studies into psychoanalize science the modern world ist answererness, that beginning twentyone century, mental health investigation are taking mental desordiers as anything. With all actual social context enfold big global crisis, accounting too social pathologies (which will spook on this book pages), Psychoanlalizys comeback in first place with the trueth above mental health investigation, ending all issues unsolving Thanks to little-understood or mishuman healthcare system. This new thougtht start because the way in how many professionals are trying find out to help children, joungs, men and women wich are shaken under sickness.

Ussualy'll get, by every reader and listener or unless to all people which are watching this text, alot Authors names invlolving down psychological and psychiatric books. But indeed speaking of Psychoanalize New School today haven't almust knowladge on this matter (at someones believe born into America in Twentyone centurys endfolding Karl Marx, National Zizialisme, Psychoanalyze and a little others theories according with keepway of to be human develop); well the question ist why? slightly thinking, could be because of so muchthings; in first place, when this text was wrote Professionals and Students were awere in that present world time lead a bigest crisis on Mental Health adressings on Human Being and His Enviroment. Who Feed! itself as mentalhealth investigation ist very, very, new. Coming soon ist time to talk of Modern Psychiatric Father the Dh. Sigmund Freud with His big and great support into psychiatric helping.

Remember that folding all psychotherapeutics men and women time across, Dh. Sigmund Freud ist the Mozzart of Psychotherapy the man which descover psychotherapy as science, away in how scientific investigations could share us a methode by ending with Issues mind. In fast, now, later evolution of psychoterapy inside differents countrys, the almust neuroscientifics and psychotherapeutics into America undertood that long time ago psychotherapy searched the manner to stop at psychopathology features or full psychopathology within psychoanalize theories and methode; because of others bunch of psychotherapy non was finding how delite mental illness, So his first goal are the goods of to be Human develop, investigation just as motivation, manpower, talents, creativity, self-actualization and so on, not syckness part of to be Human, as Earlier said.

Thanks to all unsolving issues, on America begun to born a new school from psychology this are in fast the new manner for great undesteand again in what happen with mental health on twentyone centuries, litarature and scientific investigationship. As long as ist very need remark so strong never forgot at New Psychoanalyze school are not Objetal Psychoanalyze, Child Psychoanalyze or Classical Psychoanalyze alone, but itself as new manner from psychotherapy enfold each one above this mental health investigation and studies. Searching of course scientific theory and methode, bring us an universal answer above psychoanalitic reallity taking account such culture and enviorenment (althought somebody Avoid, understeand not or clash becuase them earlier attachings hux are notted into DSM-5th Edition, 2013, p. 749-759)*22. Across pressent text´ll Be able you read more according how this new Mental Health investigation-seeks explainen us in short that antropoligy could not undertood so good psychoanalyzes because of, if make us alittle consienssousness: Sigmund Freud Text get loud remark on BIOLOGICAL facts (and say you biological in big words because of biology into psychoanalize steand envolving down psychodinamycs, joining erogen zones and/or Psychosocial stages commondly kind as far as antropology concerns).

For another part today Monday Nineteen from March in Two Thousand and Eighteen; Psychoanalyze's New School ist being writed or wrote and how on this place, in otherness world site short time ago is borned too. Perphaps someone, could talk us how was psychoanalyzes develop but here or rewardless between the next lines will remark who ist that psychoanalyzes new school born and under what nossion and vission bring us their light.

In first place ist to need gets good remind about all said over beginn text, the words Global Crisis ist reffer each more to stadistics or Charts rather in high leves wordwide when speak us for example Antisocial behaviors as killers, criminal alien, intrafamiliar issues, How mental disordiers ist enfolding on our actual system prission, and How our actual social system become our enviroment; but here the question will be in What form? Get us good answewr with this social changes? Steppen else that Psychoanalyze as science to use stadistic as the better way by get awesome asks in our investigations.

HISTORICAL CONTEXT

ECONOMIC STRUNGGLE

Time across diffent philosophys and sciences ist finding how to have great knowladge about our Mentalhealth taking variety of facts to wrap this. Thanks to it get us so much studys zones or areas: Chemic, physic, psychology, biology, and so on, by stood better To Be Human develop and social growth too. Now among vission of To Be Human, notable be studed spending one viewing alone. In this way I remember well, one saying of perseption which get the psychology as Mentalhealth area: "Among Sigmund Freud or amonsgt Sigmund Freud but never without Freud". This talking was something that classmate-inner upon to Foster over Mental Health satments.

Modern Psychiatric or Psychoanalyze new School bring lights to Psychoanalize blossoms about mentalhealth and intrapsychic-life into the Tweentyone Centurys. Yes!, to remind under timeline of psychoanalyze, itself born in oldworld doing awkward criticism against psychiatric studies, Whichever enfold interpretationship about behaviors although forget - (big mystake)- Psychiclife. With the lines noted earler, able us to put our Leader's name as for example Michel Focult, or otherness antipsychiatric theories and psychoanalizers; of course each culture get their own cutural development. But so shrewd the foster into psychiatric ahead everytime is: To end "Human being are Determined by biological upsets" same kind wichen want establishment that's someone even should be Something and noth Otherwise, because of his/her bilogical an-athomy.

Alongeside pressent theory, saw economics and socials exchange that world, in the one hand are Latin America people fluming for better further to them, utterancing what's gong on above them currency Devaluation since time ago (*1, *2, *3, *15).

Who pivote clearly, cooming soon a real dataness who exemplar statment:

1. Manuel Ávila Camacho: From $ 4.85 to $ 6.68 X 1 U.S. Dlls.
2. Miguel Alemán Valdés: From $ 6.68 to 8.65 X 1 U.S. Dlls.
3. Adolfo Ruíz Cortines: From $ 8.65 to $ 12.50 X 1 U.S. Dlls.
4. Luis Echeverría Álvarez: From $ 12.50 to $ 25 X 1 U.S. Dlls.
5. José López Portillo: From $ 25 to $ 150 X 1 U.S. Dlls.
6. Miguel de la Madrid Hurtado: From $ 150 to $ 2,300 X 1 U.S. Dlls.
7. Carlos Salinas de Gortari: From $ 2,300 to $ 3,500 X 1 U.S. Dlls. (With it the "New Peso" was initiated so the exchange rate was $ 3.50 X 1 U.S. Dlls.).
8. Ernesto Zedillo Ponce de León: From $ 3.50 to 9.36 X 1 U.S. Dlls.
9. Vicente Fox: From $ 9.36 to $ 10.88 X 1 U.S. Dlls.
10. Felipe Calderón: From $ 10.88 to $ 12.96
11. Enrique Peña Nieto: From $ 12.96 to $ 17.85 X 1 U.S. Dlls.

Appontishment this adressing in, lot of people believe than press crisis are chined over foering countrys wich win more than the same Latin America stewardship under right and left marketplace, overtaking firstly in due the secound option; In my personal opinion I believe too at same. That other folks in Latin America Countrys not will upon them incomes 'cause not care when is grasping His economic supply; maining refference to Organizations wichly send at welth Faraway from the country looking that is not accountable or quantifyed just how are Seenable on our refference(12), Than Last Single Convention of United Nation in New York March 1996(·11) the Shrinked Market leap thiefly that Mexican and Latin American Economys so thise step don't was dying but shaky because itself continued drafting economy not accountable wich others countrys far of America (countrys than hold American Political Partys who sponsors) were bigest winers while the Latin America Economy was failing, repeating again time after time same story(*3, *4). So today is good knowing the Fact for that Latin America people looks Social collapse : Human rights violations, streets everyday safeless, downess under divisa dashboard, due in a debt most complicated *35 *36 and more kinds *27 *24 *25 *26 *23 *28. Hux according wet International Standars, global standars brows protect from countrys "suffering"; coming definitions but nut are the only ones that Human Beings are scaping:

"An act causing severe physical or Mental pain or suffering; intentionally inflicted; for a proscribed purpose; by or at the instigation of or with the consent or acquiescence of a public official who has custody or physical control of the victims; and not arising from lawful sanctions"*36 *37.

(Matter of J-E-, 23 I&N Dec. 291, 297 *BIA 2002*) (8 C.F.R. § 208,18 *a*)

"Various forms of physical violence, inclunding rape, torture, assault, and beatings, amount to persecution" *38. " It can take other forms "such as the deliberate imposition of severe economic disadvantage or the deprivation of liberty, food, housing, employment or other essenstials of life" *38.

(Matter of D-V-, 21 I&N Dec. 71 *BIA 1993*); (Matter of B-, 21 I&N Dec. 66 *BIA 1995*); (Matter of N-M-A, 22 I&N Dec. 312 *BIA 1998*); (Abdel-Masieh, 73 F.3d at 583); (Matter of Laipenieks, 18 I&N Dec. 433, 456-57 *BIA 1983*)

Thise that is wrote only not is loom by Mexicans who neailer example represent. So being itself perhaps inner Thirteen currency divisa most valued on Latin America today four of March 2019(*5), among otter Nations in that Continent begun to worry. But in the oder Hand's at solving whom should leave in greatest agreetments: "prosperity to the poor", lot of sides in Latin America and otherwise worldpart aknowlegment thise statments for empowered their currency change jumping to reject Them currencys forward loud Economic investment as other Countrys.

VIOLENCE CARENESS

The tolk neailer begun becuse of activist and poll opinion spend world wide web in unmaskared a bigest Terrorist man Osama Bin Laden Leader of Al-Qaeda is alive *39 *40 *41*42*43:

"Doubts about bin Laden's death were fueled by the U.S. military's supposed disposal of his body at sea, the decision to not release any photographic or DNA evidence of bin Laden's death to the public, the contradicting accounts of the incident (with the official story on the raid appearing to change or directly contradict previous assertions), and the 25-minute blackout during the raid on bin Laden's compound during which a live feed from cameras mounted on the helmets of the U.S. special forces was cut off"*44. And meet only a picture posted websitely hux author after publish disapear at account. *39 *40 *41*42*43

And screeming than his instrusion over American Business are part of why Latin America is living in poor. In at same way Mexico is not the only one country with cheaps so, also in the North America; in Anglo America thank's to the Terror Attaks and other Crimens against Humanity (*6, *7, *8) the Goverment started to build a longest wall across sourth border *39 *15, itself could to be in at most advanced countrys in world, the further an Highest invovation into end Torrorism and Safe inocent people.

*"People are pouring into our country, including terrorists. We have terrorists. We caught 10 terrorists over the last very short period of time," -President Donald Trump- (*6)*

"We are importing radical Islamic terrorism into the West through a failed immigration system." -*President Donald Trump*- (The Atlantic Electronic Journalist Dec 11, 2018. *7)

"A convicted murderer from Honduras was arrested after illegally entering the U.S. with members of the migrant caravan, Department of Homeland Security officials said Friday". - *Bart Hansen* - (USA today nov. 30, 2018. *8)

Today the wall not is endfuly and perhaps never will happen, althought some countrys meetings tolk for step Global coperation to does immigration lacks as well*45. Another natural resources and ecologial activist fashons Speech that 'd to be a new Ecological- wall away of Human Patrimony as Symbol of Human Coperation in counter terrorism and to Wander Natural Resources Rescue (how is notted into Trumpismus chapter). Just as the great China-wall so vanguardist and Futuristic (*14 *15 *16). Forthunadly thise statments aren't lack to the Immigration facts (firstly into poor/poverty Immigrants) infeed leap new rewards to They in that Global Leadership Step a Modern Imigration system based in Stewardship Organizations supporting them as Human beings.

"There is a very good chance we can do a solar wall." -Donald J. Trump, President of the United States- (*15)

"I'll give you an idea nobody has heard about yet," Trump *told a cheering crowd. "We're thinking of something that's unique. We're talking about the southern border. Lots of sun. Lots of heat. We're thinking about building the wall as a solar wall so it creates energy and pays for itself."* - Kevyn Diaz, Chron February 2018 (*16)

Down another mean the earlier wrote isn't alone what surround our new Psychiatric Invesment or the Story from Psychoanalizes and Mental Health Statments. So, to adress more above what period of time today we are leaving; Should step at greatest -for many- victory over something wich someone would call Culture or Ideology but another belief are: "bigger barrier to the ManKind", for this have us the Science that might screen what is illness by the To Be Human Development and Social Nourish. Nevertheless March 23, 2019 (*17 *18) Journalist and another information resources scatter The victory over Slamic State (althought could reborn) or Caliphate a culture or Ideology for many people but to most insigths how for example science or quantitative agreetments is nothing about that's matter. I wouldn't bleam time talking around this because of at pressent Scientific work isn't from itself. If do you gonn to draft your own thought, suggest to you surffing information and upset your own pointview.

"Islamic State in Iraq and the Levant (ISIL)...also called Islamic State in Iraq and Syria (ISIS)" (21)

" Assad sought to portray the opposition as Sunni Islamic extremists in the mold of al-Qaeda and as participants in foreign conspiracies against Syria" *32

"In June 2014... the group proclaimed the establishment of a caliphate led by the leader of ISIL"*33

"AQI/ISI was also weakened by the loss of several of its senior leaders in attacks by U.S. and Iraqi forces". *33

"On August 8 the United States launched air strikes in Iraq to prevent ISIL from advancing into the autonomous Kurdish region of Iraq". *34

Howeven, the earlier speeched are Information so real wichly seem what's happen wet those movement that had them Gather under 2003, "Al-Qaeda in Iraq (AQI), its direct precursor"(9) and thank's to the Enforcement who at President George W. Bush and his precursor Donald j. Trump did to last several years from Human Rights Fight, today April 05, 2019 the worldwide is claming the victory from United States over that region getting peace to the affaired region, somewhat lot of people could to name to George W. Bush another American Hero wich begun that protection to end poor Humans from terrible situation and not how is suggested in at book enttiled *An Intorduction to Literature Criticism and Theory* (p.171) Howce give us to 'stood that President George w. Bush has and Hallucinatory assertion or than his put an Linguistic Aberration. Offcourse as the same author does Clear his grief is nothing objetive (At book noted before due are an greatness writing to bleam your own book are needy reckognen soon, but as Criticism is Arguirless). Futhermore at wining lauched in stilled war is enough to close thise chapter.

THE TRUMPISMUS

That philosofical statment is not our proof because of we ahead coups with Mantal Healt, seen in fast on the Psychopathological soon. Futhermore, this stametment from the today President of Homeland is akind hux jumping USA to many Historical hitos aprouching, in journey better citizens quality life that briefs most rewards by the Latin America lands also. By lot of folks could be not good undeasteanding as many others philosophers on story, where currently are hardly of understeand. But could sound wacko such maining or thinks has performing due because even must has a critizism everywhere but when pholifophy forecast in science at critizism are loudleas because by at Scietific wax at numbers lead the importnant and not otter ship. Rather the charts over Scientific investement and/or invertigations is what realy highlight.

Alongside Trumpismus, time is not many to this Human being tought inside in the world, but fastly begun to set up longer effects Dying as expample at climbing economy years earler this country and the World encounter. In abide from this granting, most lands and global organizations overtook lot of goals wich was setback or perhaps misspressent. That Philosophical Ideology is shortly gaped, like hint in advice preaching on many Human Being learningsides for example Universitys, High Schools, Empetrices, Conference of Socials above economy and enviromental development; this thinking from that president is teached in many Homeland classrooms as well as inner other World sites, by set an interpretations of what accouting that words in would at globe pin vex-less and lead to the roof top an Humanitarian Vision wich itself boost.

Whom TIME Magazine[52] said: Trump-Revolution ensure is going to change at country for ever. Such expert in that matter and Sociologyst look's like Trumpismus as Evolution from Marxist (or the correct interpretationship) sets after his secound upset on the German Nationalizm. So now into post Contemporary world, adressing in the falseness media comunications pivoten the infomation by citizens, at welth granting by end poverty, the Globalizing soon low Nationalist politcs, are some of fews maining that President cheap over such Philosophie betwixt otterness. Thereof has been well done by this and other lands in the widely for appontish in solving many vexes today mandkind ahead. Rather each more folks brows this wave forth moretime thereafther Trump time's office dying.

Thereby this is one Social, Economical and Political ideology based on macrotheory[53],[54] loomed in solving United Nations aprouchment, Agreetments nearly decades ago betwixt countrys to release Mankind from Criminal doings and Care like thise. Thereof are entilled under bigger Organisms hux United Nations, European Union, International Organization of Immigrants and so on that ills called "Human Traffiking" and "Immigrant Smuggle" are engaging this to prosper our socials, weirdly away are fixed some from this social illness World crisis coup under next Donald Trump books and others before otha as President:

Crippled America: How to Make America Great Again (2015).
The America We Deserve (2000)
Why We Want You To Be Rich (2006)

In other words thus encryptings from that Ikon of Post Contemporary world are reflexing today his Maining as Global leader doing in the press at new thinking has now than him Thrive such Nation but shrewd many otter thought flow up what's are drawing at the earth.

Psychoanalizes
in
21 Centurys

PRISION SYSTEM

Shrewd belong past, the Science was stcking the Names of people wich are investing keenly on many Matters but today for example Abraham Maslow and otherwise how's wrote around somebody called Global Leaderships or Thinkers (between more soons) and who them screem at Psychic-Life or rather what Unconsiensously journey them how Mahad Magandi and more aheaders. So psychoanalizes since Sigmund Freud until today's world even took like that High careness by itself because of never forget at professionalism. So alongside this book are stepped that Maslow teached us: "the understeanding than Psychoanalizes and Humanistic Psychology are not the same something". Likewise are expected over His Investigations wich Himself journey surrounding the twain Mental Health viewings. Pivoting as well everytime: Psychoanalizes are Sickness but Humanistic Psychology in the other hand is Healthness studies. So whole those replay us than Maslow not only did Investigation around Mental-health but in Mental-Sickness investment or investigation (in way than one Investigfation is an Investment) also. Due He and his sucessors appontishment must in waxing the Healthness or took that by fucousing their therapie pathways in Mankind, being so that Human Being when have not anything wich tramppled them life just as Mental disordiers their might alive succesfuly meet and inside them enviroment. If not, not dubt thus people should looks like one psychoanalitic orientation.

The lines wrote ago are coming because commonly Jail is a place where elsebody wich might not living healthy inside them arroundings for that need forward Correctionals or Jails. Nowhere left me step you who's were mein tripping to Homeland, where thereby begun at first psychoanalize's writing about this penitencial or correctional system.

Watching what's happen into Mankind wax on pessentime worldwide were very needy adress above our Psychic-Life for that come to me like thinking in explore at reality by traveling in this moment towards Homeland; Offcourse such opportunity bring me the naive in Explore at reality as Psychiatric Investigator or rather stud animed nor un animed objects in our social context. As scientist is what we do!

Moreover in May 2019 did what could forecast my live; in so, got at chance to award that experience life Whence sprunge me an inquiere to my mind: " how set up every country different Corrective System bunch"? Holdding thereof had at naive in stay four days under one Latin America prission --wich in short Reflex what this nation be-- a place called " The Twenty" (la veinte). Don't going to bring Detail of how Social system found Because of aren't my achievment. But been keen in how I was handcuffed granting me wet ist moment life. Well I was running because of my daily excercice in morning - surounding where myself was living, just close Homeland south border- How's got in that state a lot of troubles amongts poors for many hosts folding at Bigest Crisis wich Imigrants face in the press who adress unto ``Economic Strunggle´´ Chapter also:

"Every year, thousands of men, women and children fall into the hands of traffickers, in their own countries and abroad. Almost every country in the world is affected by trafficking, whether as a country of origin, transit or destination for victims"*27.

-United Nations Office on Drugs and Crime-

``-New United Nations data shows that a record 70.8 million people were forcibly displaced by the end of 2018 – double the number 20 years ago-´´ *24

> \- International Rescue Comitee-

``-Violence and a severe economic crisis have shattered the lives of millions of Venezuelans. With extreme hyperinflation gripping the country many are no longer able to afford food, rent, transportation or medicine. Hospitals are short of qualified staff and are scaling back provision of health services. They no longer have access to the drugs and supplies they need, forcing them to require patients to bring even medical gloves with them if they wish to be treated-´´. *25

> \- International Rescue Comitee-

``-El Salvador provides the most compelling evidence of this, where it is estimated that in 2014 the poverty rate would have been 12 percent higher without those remittances. Another analysis conducted in Guatemala using data from that same year demonstrated that the likelihood that a family would face food insecurity decreases by 40 percent when it receives remittances-´´. *26

> \- World Bank -

``-The socialist-driven economic and humanitarian crisis ravaging the beautiful country of Venezuela should give every American pause. It is not just that this ideology, which has failed the people of this South American nation, is now establishing a footing here in the United States—but it's also because our beacon of hope that shines throughout Latin America is being threatened by America's adversaries-´´.*23

-Kimberly Guilfoyle-

``-Between 1980 and 2015, the number of migrants from this subregion who were living in the United States increased by an annual average of 8 percent and in 2017, their total number in the United States stood at close to 3 million. Most persons leave because of the shortage of good jobs, high rates of crime and violence, and the desire to be reunited with their families-´´. World Bank say *28.

-Axel vang Trostsenburg-

That morning mainwhile excercices a policewomen cometh to me
for deceive myself not been people from its state & whom my
ID was in the living-home as long as making mein health
careness, were unable identify front at woman.

To do so send me towards "The Twenty" (La vente) one
Detencion Center where whosoever Immigrants and other soon
insteand, somebody because alive over street nor for them
immigration situationship nor for being don't highest Criminal or
wears not antisocial Behaviors. Thise neive leave me know
Homosexual drives into Jails envolven fixations on phalic, oral
and anal stages. Where they how conciensously or unconciensouly
inner to the prision to set this behaviors and refiel the anxietys
how's coming from libidinal pultion, psychic energy, or ID, into
Dying needs of pleasure or sometimes Bliss. Ist for so when I
was overthere flourish on me mind greatest statments, a Theory
wich perhaps otherwise thought too in the Eairler: "When goes
currently by Jail or Correctional Centers are chained Personality
Disordier wet Eudiphical stage in Criminal or Antisocial
Behavior"! Been the inquiere What's face our prisioner or
consultant about that? Them personal and social story holding
(familiar story) how are stepped! Due modern world puts not
Homosexual Behaviors as Mental Disordier in some bunch
(suggesting them could or not wears nexts disordiers in that
code but even comorbing otherwise) :

CODE: 302.85 (F64.1)

``This chapter employs constructs and terms as they are widely
used by clinicians from various disciplines with specialization in
this area. In this chapter, sex and sexual refer to the biological

indicators of male and female (understood in the context of reproductive capacity), such as in sex chromosomes, gonads, sex hormones, and nonambiguous internal and external genitalia´´.

``The need to introduce the term gender arose with the realization that for individuals with conflicting or ambiguous biological indicators of sex (i.e., "intersex"), the lived role in society and/or the identification as male or female could not be uniformly associated with or predicted from the biological indicators and, later, that some individuals develop an identity as female or male at variance with their uniform set of classical biological indicators´´.

``Disorders of sex development denote conditions of inborn somatic deviations of the reproductive tract from the norm and/or discrepancies among the biological indicators of male and female ´´.

(DSM-5, 2013, p. 451)

As well as our duty how Psychoanalizt is leap Jail recidents to aim them wichen could suffer some adaptation pathway over social commitments. In thus situationship are needy attach therapy flow wether over conciensus or unconciensus psychic life level. In other words in the willing must descover us a lot of cases get's awere about what I foretold. So in otherwise them are unknoweth above the matter.

Howsoever your therapeutic orientationship shall you adress like that as Psychoanalizes wrote on this pageswork by better patient understeanding. To continue meet my surffing naive thereafter to be outside of "La Veinte" (the twenty). Are needy pull than whence enjoy Homland myself walked to Border Patrol officails reseaching aid by my new live traveling. Them as soon as setted me unto few Detention Centers or correctional meet foerings folks from that country. Afterall last being longer time on Jail look's like each one are so Diferent. On one hand upon Higynless Center's Country in Latin America, and whom Mental Health proffesional were showable bigger difference betwixt wether. - Before to continue are needy to do Clear that this modern Psychiatric writings blossom over this Chapter regards both Mental health Institutions meet another Correctional Center and also Personal psychiatric cases. - In the Oder hand like this are nor the same outstanding (the jails). Mailwhile Homeland's correctionals flux must freedom by them prisioners. Into Latin America wich keeps same people bunch but freelessness, been wheter same inmate levels.

Alongeside mein thougts don't get doubt In wealth-power are pivoting what's Going on above thus. So itself is somehow we not will surffing in that book. But in both mankind holders are so easy seek where folks stick more freedom getting must resources acces. For example the "Twenty" (la veinte) get's rooms or cells woso twelve men have place to slumber, sleepin two men in each bed within three cup-soup daily to food (an aweak to Human being developness). As long as the Jail at another country has such cells take place by unless one hundred people, each one wet them owner bed to slumber, between technology resources, gameboards, telephones, free choice eat, snack shopping and lo.

Nevertheless this mainwise biologicaly and cognitive wax overwhelming not in same levels. Thereafter were so needy know every kind by our next adressing that ist at firstly item attached under this Chapter. Nowhere get us knowledge than Homosexual Personality features are linked to Criminal behaviors. Polling that in the roof top of Psychiatric dutys how is: "Become slowly selfperception concerning consultant to him will has bestest agreetments with whole that himself is and wet the around He are facing". Meet all thus foretold you at firstly achievement is set gladness in our consultant but sometimes could be easy not do that. Sampling as wheel the Why them currently leave Criminal thrivers to shake on Prission in relief what their Libidinal Instint they believe feed, commonly going or fixed to another behaviors nothing above of solving their sexuality needs Consiensously. For that our consultalnt could unconciensouly away dying them Libidinal Instint in perverse forms associed to his neave of live: childhood, parental relationship, thinkgs of them future, teen age, and indeed at minds their parent flow about he or she before birth.

Overtaken Psychoanalizes lights thus uncounsiensous and consiensous mainings them journey, Firstly been at most important ones before anything, the relationship wet their primary social context where they beloved object yield less pleasure or bliss. Futhermore them dumy other beloved object wich could wish uptown in Sadic way without take important their "idealized father" or "father gosth" the social Laws that could be or not there, howsoever them must do such and each host to uptown the wished object. This object on symbolic lingo could be animed on unanimed but even in at mental paint from everyone than object reflx and expect diferent host and pin pon from the Psychotic by the psychopass and/or sociopass behaviors.

Therein our consultant, inmate or patient might not solve thereof from himself, likewise at Mental living real or unreal could even forecast in a new psychical or physical simptum. Overall just here are needy aknowledgment than at highlighting on Wished object are not chained only to one Eudiphical complex stage everyone fix them own psychic life on different or differents stages*46 *47 Psychoanalizes on twenty one Century clash also meet classical viewing form mental health been thus olders or news, itself are because of Psychonalizes reckogn Mental stipwardship own consultat suffer in reality or over Guess draft fastly synaptics conexionship betwixt neuro transmisors hux even might damage in the way at brain throw longer time or not, on Oxipital, Parietal, Frontal or Temporal cerebell zones, doing symptoms and sings. Our duty must need adrees that too.

THE NEW ID

Dr. sigmund Freud puts bibliacal Verse inner him Psychoanalizes commitments and paperworks thus don't dubt are because down Wersten Culture Jew-Christianism lead social rullings throw many years before. Mein wise are hux someone by this book too.

"After six days Jesus took with him Peter, James and John the brother of James, and led them up a high mountain by themselves. There he was transfigured before them. His face shone like the sun, and his clothes became as white as the light". -Mattew 17:1-2-

Time latter today's world fluming somehow such apparently click thise kind in the same manner but perhaps or sometime trougth out another methodology. Setting a little whole I'm gonna foretold you is how Psychiatric or Mental Health developer post the earlier Biblical verses because of issues we ahead reflex us and is rejected even by the external soon. Being ourselves like window of Majesty or aweakness.

Are just since the Gather look's like how Icons from at must extensive and reprentatives mind-healing matter at the world could get, Names as Sigmund Freud or Soren Kienkergard harvest wich still Biblical handencrypting also. Rolling like that transfiguration story appear ever Jew-Christian hallowed Scriptures. Raisen dwell Jesuschrist screenself His Face whom Never before as Sunshine flashing. Moreover mankind would plot what Jesus stepped in his own Because of was Human being too. Thereof I'm endeavoring of lay out its Truthly a Same host that's happend into Psychoanalizes seassion. Myself nodded at time in whose semblant's consultant forecast latter of psychoanalizes twice like that.

Leaving meet itself Jesuschrist fits great Halthness by people, Healing soon their time beside. Being him Preacher and explorer one. For so mankind or rewardless werstern culture upon Jew-Christian Holly writtings as wheel. Now to adress consultant cheaps be keen than spend few tools come nessesariosly & is goodness, Psychoanalizes howsoever might blem that.

Weackness and weep mankind get's Mainwhile they alive Daily. For that is, Why Him begging one psychoanalizes nor otherness health mind prosses! Wherefore we as care's folder pin pon proof commands to aid everyone come by us. Throw therapeutic time looking for the weeper or may consultant are showable only not them smell or laugthing but whole their face forecast (inclunding their body too) In other words truetly become.

Lo, let me say thus aren't somewhat on therapy appear alone, catching itself unto more to be Human pathways too. As for example when goes like church or when step up something than last enforcemet of endeanvoring uptown so, when you sing at the Church to fix hints by descover yourself or allowed you felt better meet your deeps. Nevertheless Psychoanalizes shut thereof by thus facing pathologys hux disordiers or may be transtor them live, getting a specific tratment by such one and plot at marry our consultant even wise too alive.

Boot, how could us be awere in what's up within our consultant or client? have an physiological viewing? a kind watch us to observe at answere our patient upon? At replay is, yes! like Jesus we migth seek us too how's apparience client or weeper cheap for otterness. First: must our client or sicked became at bunch them eyes are colored, the light (but an internal light coming from the patient non of external stuff) must be different clearing themselves. Seconth: their head apparience must leap different too adressing on them factions in other words could seem as unreckognezable. Third: His voice must till other soon not in the way than before psychoanalizes. Commondly that voice patient could be different, in feed has even a lot of tone voice but I don't remark such melody, mein appontishment are more in why his vibes cover us, even has voices from folks wich sound sick like this are because in at same manner eyes reyect us at loftiness that people living more than color voice or temperature is above the healthness transfer in his wave by the attent psychoanalizer. In at next booking will grant a chapeter more around the voice.

Shutting this chapter book perhaps somewhat could discrebe that as razist but not way althought such and each becamigs foretold lines ago will be press in every consultat we done on, offcourse in gradueal manner gaping as well the Therapy time will have, at pathology to coupe, and at tratment must needy being that baffled or not.

TRANSFERENCE

Saturday 19, Junuary 2019

Last my nears experiment that's doing to the social emviroment, undertaking whys and hows in get lacks off, any thougth forecast whats seem to myself the around in at Daily, so when someone did a Hub wich has linking to like video on Psychoanalitcs such as well thinking gether to command me instand: "whom tranferens as psychic leave hold Telekinetics*49 (psychic power) and Telepathy*48 that's picks resources from our own space-staff (facts of Frequences in psychic energyc as some authors preffer tolk to them, does beating in the long space or stay fluxeen an sub-athomic waves on otherness whom over molecular paths of something playing as thriving to swtch up the nearly uptowned in that message or psygessment), whel surffing up-on Getting like that.

Thursday 26 September 2019

The whole notted ago were wrote months before my traveling to Homeland whom explain on a chapter named "Prisions systems" today ending this literacy work took that I shall did but might not because of the findings by issues goverment on this country stumbled me. Time latter been jailed on Homeland backward to my House again mainwhile Homeland are hoping like paperworks me should send up by holding me within fits from the wrongs and Human Right violations at country I living is suffering. Hearth damage were plucking mein own when descover than at same country in how I living browsed at Mail ship, hux share to Homeland, in does once more ill things thise countryes plot amongst them citizens. Dubt nay ist than if I not was smitted is because all callings made by otters lands like more flock push the same in jumping to another life quality or dissapears from opression countrys as foretold into Chapters back. At thought spruning mein is look's like the way in recover my tripping done card or VISA same than missed because this -"in highest criminal, poverty, human right broucks and immigrant level"- nation wears squirring in my maining unallowing the same than most country speech: "we are not bleaming no kind amonst none". Wait that's countrys can learn on and flip flop the thiefness hux set up against their ones. Howsoever them progress must be longer but latter will talk why. Nowhere is O'Clock by seen about Transference.

Who is leap alonside fristh lines, ship than Transference is like phenomena folding telemagnetism, away of telekinesis or telepathy. Such phenomena might been throw slightly or longer distance, in otter words can't even or nesesariously bin closed at the object, whereas object might be a fantasy, an idealization from the reality as well as something than never or not exist rewardless under external ego's world althought cloud in the further exist. Perhaps like this could gather norm kinds or an doing by the ego wich not must distress itself getting on him a heathly way of living. Boot when doesn't so this transferece could leave neurotic or psychotic ego outsdatanding in don't uptown from that object at pleasure ego's fluming. Therein whence ego are lacks of witholding will looks at difused ego blissing the object and lossing the ego's deffences dessaperaing at ego indeed seeming the false ego rather: "at object diffuse itself or in many time splinter him".

So I would stick more at the physical prosses wrasping Transference, an electromagnetic one our mindset cheap over sub-athomics agents itself fly around space in to link to other animed or unanimed object. Such transference should be at each object in the wide but discriminatory prosses*50 *51 take at object must commonly unconciensously income by the ego as well. As example someone get's his or her partner-love and one picture of he or she, at descriminatory pivot grants in what object shall be transferenced loudly and that less. Thus electromagnetism gathering from mental one smash up time after time atomics matter surrounding space in wave effect. Due have not only one trasference procces hux main in that way. Anotter Transference flow araise from the speaking in the daily. For example when someone are speeching meet otherness at same noted above must occur but nowhere talking prosses or rather at vibe overwilling the mounth and the voice ("voice is a concept harved under Psychoanalizes in twenty one century that well display you chapter full in the coming") on wheter is broad a sound instand sub-moleculars punch betwext themselves althought such noise are not heared throught out Mankind ears.

Thereof could screen something very absurd and unable by the Science or regardless to the science yieled at the General public speaking yet in at press twenty one centurys. For that would yield you at naive myself liveth beside Homeland tripping. Just whom Explain chapters before, I was Homeland towards in avoid lot of thing must happend amongst me now I understeand than otherwise could forced the threathers and harmers (violents agents of Lands) because of foering interest and perhaps lot of Nations are suffering the same, forced to do the unavoidable wichen is explained on Historical Context Chapter, as Imigration business where is most pro fitable to the goverment bring anykind at citizens in that itself begging their going until otter lands by the foering interest wich main the same govermet uptwon throw pilgrims network greatest incomes. In other words "I (the foreing Interest mainig governess) given't no kind to you but want from you high pursiut to forwarding you by otter Nation.

Howsoever months latter brows up aid in the neibor country Got on my mind at voice from a woman of than country framtime but the uncanny is than never was hearing such voice, every night when slumber at voice from that woman, hux work by this neibor country, pin pon my head strongly. Suddenly after lot of time ramdomly this voice my sleeping was brought and fastly give up from the bet araising me forward the door of my housing, in the time I'm outside in the Street into private block of houses a waith car is begin his runing until wherever. But when look's like enjoy that car the same woman hux endeavored fix comunicationship trought out meanstream were upon automovil one. Was unable speeching with her beacuse of the goverment did whole in them hands had by not get succes in my traveling. How notted in the earler, due if not were gap any talking within otherwise land could be die today.

But Just there is what we want nearly explain in phenomena tilled transepherence verythere a prosses like telepaty. Rather that typing physical making Transpherence, are needy attach: traspherence is currently unconciensouly and when not ever wears something unconsience away.

As well as transepherence might not been in emotions alone or Psychic content but from knowladge also. To Explain so slim the next must show whom can us get acces at collective mind. By been most keen must puts the next withnessess: "Kevyn M." other fictinal name by protect at man hux we are talking He is Student and surrently get's good job. "Kevyn M." explain how wereable descover at identity from some criminals dangerus in whole the Globe, they are at sponsor from fews terror atack against Humanity. On this writing are very clear how trancepherence leap an important roll. And is so easy understead most if you as professional wears Psychological trainig.

After lot of talkings in at moment terror attacks were boomed in Homeland 9/11, About at leader which promove thus hurting "him never was punished" and that criminal "were hided in at country nation insteand must close" from at victim's land. This same matter birth up in a political class him got on Public University, searching acts of political mains, Him latter of get in his knowledge how ideological groups or Religion's team currently persecute or harass otherness than aren't from at same faith*55,*56,*57 and Mainwhile his mind journey at insight in who uncanny way the people bleming at Terror attack (in Homeland) are the same religion of this Ideological's team than harass other religions on same country, and at most inportant the same state in at country where this religions are moust populed are the state in such political class tolk is hided such Criminal. In other words thus criminal was hided in one state his Ideology or Religion are bigger and later descover that state promove persecution of this religion against somebody. Him foretold his Human Right were brought pivoting International grantings and conventions, curiosly in at similar maner are speeched on Historical context chapter in this hurtness amongst heself him be awere than they are members (human roght violators) of same Religion noted above, the religion of Criminals hux are equals to the Religions the state political Classmate in university scroll. Is overthere just when hux psychic process dispay at reality and at collective mind can be readed! Kevyn yield he had coup mit that issues afther failing many trys for that begun brows informationship and throw that information seen keenly in a picture this criminals (the terrosit in 9/11) are the same harass some folks (Human Rights Violators) My recomendation were be highly care when bring at information by authority. Trancepherence is an procces withdrawthing instint and otter knowledge buch sometimes thogether other times nop.

PSYCHOANALIZES FROM CONTEMPORARY WORLD

Latter of the Humanistic Mental Health Investment focoused not over Pathology or raither under Human Being Health, not in at Sickness. Today Birth most investment based from the Sigmund Freud Therorys and His Contemporarys Men and Women, Adressing into the Why? Appontishment on the Pathology! Resent Studys also enfold our social context, the Laws, The Authority figure, The colective mind, the Cultural develop or growthup all Academic Draw. Althought psychoanalyzes till over have a Scientific methode and professionalism these studies won't take the Academic matter how the Only knowladge zone to work, but If psychoanalizes attachment in otherness To be Human means, these never want to loss the Scientific factor. However, in the one hand Getting a vision of To be Human wich Can not seek the psychogensis how drivers or behaviors is leave on our Social enviroment and in the Persons as Humans.

Nevertheless under psychoanalizes on 21 Centurys adress in a kind entilled Social pathology itself would gap at social enviroment only not to hold Human being weeps but to leap at social context in set up pathways to prevent, reduce and heal what socials lead at the Mankind to the sickness. Thus social pathology has been seek timeline in To be Human story. For example theroes currently ending on the mutilation of socials, in many time a sadic behavior against our arounding, in otter soon most passive. This social pathology due are chained meet at thinking-self each surrounding or social groups (ethnics, races, religions and so on) wears betwixt that, the superego and/or ideal of ego. Althought at ego perseptionship from the external world or called to by many authors the object's word flum up his own psychodinamic is a general law but every Culture allow or switch on what drivers highlight or what others not. For example Hara-kiri[*58],[*59] on Oriental cultures trougth the years was something perhaps whorty by at warrios slay heself and hurred by them enviroment, and by us as Health Care professionals, going on by suicide is psychopass maining[*60],[*61],[*62] So maybe at lawly thus warrios pick could therin granting that but itself avoid not at dinamic's ego every human has in at world like kind none is outside in the way.

At noted example is some from at social pathologys when the charts is highly. Thus could face the collective mind[*64] (the social pathology) amongst at rules, provoken disordiers in context as over our Mental beings. In other words an collective Eudiphical complex endenvoren slay what them believe or understeand is their father or at father gess they have, because could look's like this collective a father hux real is not. Watching a Little bit the psyhic prosses Collectives draft mainwhile itself sometime is with awereness other times is not.

Futhermore Due our Scientific viewing take a way other influence firstly offcourse from Dr. Sigmund Freud and his learners. Common less we take so slightly of The NAZI ideology without doubt we are not holding or fostering Xenophobie. Before continue done, are needy attach, at reality today we are living are different, the Mankind Thought are otherwise than Nazismus time or in the other hand from his Influence the Marxismus. On this book not must adress details lofty, due in our other Literacy work. Howsover whats Psychoanalizes is above Sociology? well inner Psychoanalizes 21 Centuries undertake what Karl Marx and Adolf H. fought, hux are at maining from a tilled Elitism this social class wich upon over otherwise appontishment on this situationship in at Psychological development from the other social class directly and indirectly away, and whom deform at Mental health them get's. Stiffneked or not there is something that whole Universitarian or rewardeless knowledge finder be awere, it is called social consiparationship. In at same buch that Storical icons has been understood not good, blaming ills or lacks of interpretation. Remember us that thus flocks firstly Marx sougth him theory by granting the poor, thereafter Adolf. H. explain us that Marxism was spend by to do something than is indeed anti-marxist saying that for example artist, goverment and other privilege class are danger by the Social growth and Health and the Controll them has over socials is anti-marxism full.

Such kinds are not important less by us because towards whom found our Social enviroment and at maining itself upon in Mankind or regardless in our patient is something worthy from analyzes in the way than we want, wrasping human being, at the better by himself. Yielding also could psychoanalizes gap Social context too in otters investments and jobs in account from studies and intervination. In abide of this statmatment must show how our appointing are not justify what Adolf H. did for example (althought in our next book will sling in to the wall of trueth than has folding this matter, lot of thing are far from judge people: relationship betwixt Freud and Him, the False death of NAZI leaders, at diferent versions above whats going on. Howso at story part never tolk), but will draft sharp at socio historical context owner consultant ahead and due what external ship could maing his life wheter animicly and unanimicly bunch.

Everything wrote earler Remind me a man called "James" (as you know that story are real but not at name in rebel nay at patient Identity) Him brows out Psychoanalitic pathway because of anger such thing him performe like hubbe but offcourse one Catetized object by he "His Object of love" dissapered suddenly not in a time but in a many times occured so. him in stress less or economic's ego juerney set up me this living a kind snap him, very grief he were than His Mental Health could be disage because thereof. Under Psychoanalitic methode him diceive Paranoidism and me if were not awere about what this chapter screen due mein diagnosis shall be unless allusinatorian concernes. Neurosis cheap to the Psychos when conffece me him tought slay himself. All psychiatric or regardelss when hear that pin pon that consultant roll play psychopass behavior where at ending from all sickness even is at Death. Psychoanalitics tools aid him in care and safe his ego loudly each mechanic defence by the real ego death not.

Alongside therapy when I believe him suffer delirium-persecution and that his mental states were shortly before suicide an Schizofrenic living. My first duty were barried the suicide than after time was succes him found otters aims in his live were forecasting slowly. Therin I understeand than whole he said was real and me seemed Human been story even are people impeached for spend the propertys from otherwise & them own name particular case of copy-right and to do so. Due that is whats Adolf H. suggest when say at preority someone in the arts and Governess has and how them might pivot opression amongst otter folks. How healthly is that by our enviroment. How many suicide situationship are holding the same So should this social control (or whom you want called like that) set up in the likelyhood from one person and in one manner alone? Shrewd it than utterence you is something that scatter many people and in different soon even not abroading suicide but other illness by the Mental Healt could upon. Sigmund Freud Humanistic one wich in his time reserched get queerness into Mankind because of Biological Determinations such context had, up set first than any other kind Human Being well is always Psychoanalitic achievement.

As General culture will fix more above that matter, for example at bigger lie or stricky than Marxismus is againt Studies betwen more. Is not our Goal talks or soport any Ideological or political opinion but nesesariulsy know thereof. Because our realy adressing is the To Be Human goodness Mentaly appointing. So this chapter enfold at influence privilege groups or class coup in others Mental Health.

SOCIAL INFERIORITY COMPLEX

Psychoanalizes new School or American psychoanalyzes took the conspiration theriory by attach in The social development and Human Being Growthing. Were for example how the person is determided to a social context and the culture is advocating what behaviors or drivever gets or not, in the same way what paths bring to every person in our enviroment by derterminig the personality. For example have two forms of people, some christians and others not (to suggest something), wich are living in a culture where only fews person can to do the spionage agaist other person how special rewards. Doing more clear might oder sampler: One rap-grup have special support than others authors that not have, the rap grup within press support might to spionage the other authors stealing their property, the rap for don't be Chirstian (or otherwise) have acces to other tecnology and soon in watch the thinking that other people feels. Inferiority complex might be in Colective form how enjoyn a Grup rap or between colectives or social organization wich don't bring the same paths for be or not from one religion, philosofical thinking or Society and altought been covered migth that special rewards flux a sadic behaviors amongst wich haven´t. How many care them socials wising external object to recover ego´s need in the firsth viewing because if lofthy slightly could us discover more.

Analizes us fastly the Rap grup, What doesn't their special supportiong that need enjoy on the personal life that other people, Selves at not have the same special support. What effect gets those over our social enviroment in matters as economic, cultural growthest meet otherness. Whatching too, What meinning over Bell-Curve draft only not on a Rap-Grup (as example), unto Human Being Growing or Relationship Lands Between. This think surffing in thougth about Why Sigmund Freud and Karl Marx peraphs are the must influencial men in neo-contemporary world. Today their viewing, whole is misunderstendable in an percentment.

Into other part be the Gruop or colective which felth, talking on theory (and opening hypotesis) that his need of pleasure is delayed for an External Object, but what's reason in fall colective, organizations or group mechanism defence wich commondly weeping themselves or their external objets and enviroments.

PARANOIDIMS UNTRUETH

Talking about develop personality or foster, currently think us for example in Family environment. Enfolding psychoanalyze theories to be Human ist determined within social environment not biological within as anothers authors suggest. If remember us a little Sigmund Freud to share his theory with biological vision as Professional and Darwinist Influence, in other words perhaps Sigmund Freud was one man involved into big Global Revolution for his knowledge about Mentalhealth studies and investigation, but remember us that only not get us pressent man into Mentalhealth studies and investigations theories whichever suggest as Michel Foucault, Erick Ericksson, Donald Winnicott and more.

Likewish this literature as each literary job story across bring us opportunity by better to be Human growth because thinking a little and remind else, Psychoanalyze born enjoy Humanity vision in the world, ending with perverse To be Human Studies and xperiments that unfortunately today stand working yet. But thus lines don't are by talk about many ways of mishuman xperiment, but with at Humanity vision that Psychonalyze enfold, Will be almust clear if to share next experience.

First, before to speech of this new theory, will want suggest you great book entitled "Sólo Vine a Hablar por Teléfono" from Latinwritter Literature Nobel Prize winner called Gabriel Garcia Marquez. His book ist big criticism by Actual Psychiatric System where The people spend all their time and economy in something than never was trueth, aslo ist tremendous criticism in how Social sytem when determined To be Human Personality and not the Biology, Rather, could understeand that biology get little percent and Social Enviroment take other big part or big percent into to be human foster and personality develop.

However with this introduction ist time to seek another story with intentionship of Take more knowledge and to feel what's feeling our case into consult or Psychoanalytic process. Asgard ist the name in how will be called our young. Asgard is Mentalhealth student in a particular university in state to him. He begginned to take impression that someone ist ever back to him, as following to he. And in shorttime was to talk with his University Mentors. Called cellphone within psychopathologycal miss to him and never get and answer, also searched his Master woman for to share whole ist living, of course that never to said according with Asgard what been issues supply. But is clear at his Masterwoman never questioned him about this matter, in time when Asgard said all of people back him since time ago the Miss answer him saying: "I believe at you're Paranoid" an answer so offencive by him.

Could to suggest that before to say something to our coustumer our patients for example ever ist get on mind that our job ist understead to they. Enfold Disordier Stadistic Manuals and otherness of Dx, seem us that Asgard could to get Paranoid Disordier but this never been real, Why? easy he made many pics and save all email where enjoy others states into this same time his privasity been perturbed and each pic was evidence that of course some persons been back he.

As well as nessesariouly ist don't to do thus mistakes ways and remind Sigmund Freud (Modern Psychiatry Father) Prhase "All Psychology ist Social Psychology" in other words each society and environments get their own HealthCare concept (but among the science ist so easy get a Quantitative answer). On this Psychoanalytic Literature or Scientific Investigation seem us that

Asgard real story and Gabriel Garcia Marquez book has big relationship, in first place over actual psychiatric system criticism. For example the woman in Gabriel Garcia Marquez Book lived terrible issues about Schizophrenia Hallucinations among, that never been real, the whole book suggest perverse conspiration against she by to win great economic reward and bring false answer until the husband Saying "Your wife get many Mental Disorders, but don't worry we can help to she". In others words as xpert people ist Psychiatric institute how have the "reason" her Husband gave us impression of Ignoranceman.

The woman and Asgard not got the same luck, Woman was declared among madness and Asgard never speaked with anybody of how been all this issue, or how beggined it, but spended thus strategy about pics and to save all evidence by unallow that someone will say that he has some Mental Disorder. Now in other tittles writhed time ago I suggest how ist so Dangerous seek Psychoanalyze as Philosophy because not are, Each people at believe Psychoanalyze as Philosophy ist ending with the whole objectivity whichever be «Ego Protect» or «Mind Healing», rather, Psychoanalyze ist to be human relief ever.

TWO KIDS AUTISMUS AMONG

One mother have a DX that Doctorwoman gave to she, when the mother be with her Boys on a clinic, obioussly she Beggin to have sad feels, so DX was Autismus in her Two Kinds.

The Mother Knew this DX when her Childs had six years old. The new was so very hard by his adopthative father because of in the Moment when he Knowed it, his Reaction was in treuth Sad. Indeed he feeled Need from Talk with his wife by say to she that the relationship ist Break.

In this Story the Film don't explain children's life between 0-6 years old, yet possible is not view all family's history, Relation NatalFather-Mother for example, or father-sons relationship and so on.

It Sound in my Head as: whats Living thus Boys when his parents Breaking? What was the Point by their Breaking? How was Relation father-mother?

Last all, the School Propose at mother one psychiatric Institut, but before it the mother's sons was searched Support on anothers Institutes. A Few Days latter one state's Agent was to view at mom's childrens, as Special help. He Never Spoke with the mother's above her Personal life, or her passt, Relation with her Hausband and more for example.

The Boys yet have six years old, and state's Agent beginn to Teach for How speak, Write and more. Is simple view this cognitive behavior Labor. But with all it, I don't can Belive that he Never to did another way of Intervention. Alot Days passed, the Boys learned very so much and so good.

Well, when the children become in yungs, Thanks to all work they abled learn Must activities. End.

Three Notes.

1.- Mother donot is to simple view Phatological Woman her Aspect is Natural and heatly.

2.- Thouth the boy in film non See, If their lived one psychoanalilys, it don't Could be possible because of when children's DX was reveled, they had six years old. And in this age they don't Speak, for the Phatological condition, as well as to do free asossiation ist impossible.

3.- Here also we can view: down First years old from live from thus kinds Must probabily they had and Lived aussent father. Heselves abled Support mental develop of his Childrens? Was Phatological father? His behaviors was to become Fantasy on Reality?

In and Must inquires Touch our Hears when when See us the Film but don't is possible answerer it, because of non have all the information.

For end as better can be, yet and only, I can say: Story Ended in they Growthen and Married. Well, I Hope my Essay Could help you in something.

Thanks.

PSYCHOANALIZES ADRESSING

Short time ago, indeed little days ago a few women inquire me above why the psychoanalyze is offenive by the person that is taking this process or why psychoanalize will can be ofenssive, also thus women question me from else psychoanalitic process could be depressive too.

When the words of thus women touch my ears, my psyche beginned to have alot reationships. the first answer that can gave to they was: "The psychoanalyze don't have as goal be ofenssive with anybody, maybe the persosn that is taking psychoanalitic process could feel -in psychoanalitic terms- Unpleasure, of curse is normal feel unpleasure when our "I" steand or feel danger for an external context".

But the Psychoanalyst need to have all skills an professional growth by not make at psychoanalized feels offended or else depressive. Likewise sometime is hard understood that psychoanalyze ist not a play; some once could be Funny the 'insigth' ' but is not ever. I end my answer saying for remember they that "The psychoanalyzes don't have as goal be offensive with anybody never, and when don't understead it, is not good for to do a psychoanalityc process".

Above if this process can be depressive, my secoud answere was as Otto Kernberg say: "Psychoanalyzes is not Philosophie because is a Science and could be very danger if is taked as Philosophie".

Thereafter other ones ask myself if psychoanlizes might be by all bunch folks but mein ansewere was NOP duely because as wrote before this words Psychoanalizes is even by psychopatologys or sickness commondly by healing that so if some people wix consult at psyconalizes prosses is all his right, in at same therapeutic time must dicorver if are better be granted by otter therapeutic pathway. So here you Like reader and professional or studentd from that matter, has you this knowledege and when come by you don't deny none your hearing or time if are available truethly.

BAD DIAGNOSIS

By don't reveled the name about woman that was bad Dx of an Hospital, and the Hospital names having on account his Identity, only to do us reffer at his adjetives, But here ist so big important give know from it's a real history, and as first goal ist recognized that though today have us big technological and scientific advance, the bad Dx is yet, viewing it as one Health Care issue.

In my last days I was living on Citynorth of this land and had opportunity from highlihts with the people that go at his Hospital and stead with they day and nigth, supporting with motivation by be must strong front his familiy's syck. All was in this Hospital in Citynorth of country.

Well, was by me amazin how the people can win at syck being more psychological strong. This last line maybe could be big support by New Investigations about. Continuig with the bad Dx: one night a woman comeon them Hospital because many months ago had more than 40ºC from temperature, all was for eating something that was so Bad for She.

Afther that medicine's proffecionals solving her issue above Eatintoxication and temperature, her BioPsychoDX was without depression and problem with her impultions controll. Acording with this Dx she have not impultion controll and for it medicine's proffetionals give to She psychiatric alophatic therapy.

Of course around the world psychiatric drugs are & have so Bad famus. When the woman had her alophatic therapy answer, she never thinked in take the psychiatric drug. Why?, maybe she thinked in beginn psychiatric drug dependece, obioussly on finding her own health care, search otherness alternative therapy was so better by the woman.

She is a yung woman has 20 years old only, of so much time ago has a religiouslive, when I speak with she his own words was " I don't never taked the psychiatric drug because could be dangerous by me" and What happend with you tonight, you is so good? -was my inquire-, oh yes, catholic religious woman give me great therapy agaist depression - answerer me. Oh realy I can see your BiopsychoDx? -was my secund question.

When taked in my had her Dx the first that can viewed was that She never had depression acording them Dx. I give otherness inquieres to she about, why taked a therapy against depression if do you not have depression?, and why religiouswoman which gave you therapy, never watched that do you have not depression if on Dx say it?

Before of continue, I want to do big Warnig by all people that have Mental Health issue, I understood the religious people goods intations, but ist alot importan that the people at give therapy will have all skills by can interpretationship one Dx, or of less understeand what's the issue with consultant.

Now the nigth in I knew at Woman, I question to She too, Why come on at Hospital again. "Well the last week, in peregrinationship for not safe me, had temperature again but now is -Bronchitis- and come on for view what happen with me because don't can remember manythings so good from my first Hospitalizationship variousness months ago".

Her Behavior was as if she could have big assienty as if her "I" missed the controll over her "Id or IT". She was very impultionship only. Afther from a few medicine's professionals intervinationship she was Hospitalized with forceshirt. Here have us an available question Why? She needed an answere about what's happen with her memory.

Now for ending this chapter, why medicine's professionals taked the idea of to use a forceshirt. How medicine's professionals take the first Dx about "impultions controll" as trueth. They not knew if She was equal before her eatintoxication, maybe his impultion controll not have nothing to view with the temperature because acordig at her father Sher ever was impulsiveness woman.

ALOPATIC THERAPY CONSECUENCE

Past weeks I writed above how bad PsyDx could be very dangerous by Person if not is good maked, the before Chapter see us how a yung woman hurt poor Dx cocecuense. Now on thisliness will take a exelent example from it big issue. Well, in present essay will talk of a woman which got between theertyfive years old more or less, She never had the knowladge that a psychiatricman maketh bad job trying of heal her problem.

Indeed maybe the psychiatricman never had the knowladge that He did this mental support withoutgreat answer, because by He, his job is take Disourder Stadistic Manual and to do his DX. Or maybe actual Healthcare System today don't gave us good services, I don't say that be bad Healthcare System, in others words ist an obsolet Healthcare System alone.

Is time to start to speak more about this woman. All beginned a morning when I was giving my socialservices or volountier as Theater class inside CECEM (institute that gave social support as art class, karate, futball, consuelor, agroteaching and more) when walking on this Institute front me was a woman which she needed speak with me in fast, because She is wathing if could inside into my Theater class, and also said me that needed to do more excercice as bodytherapy.

When I hear it my first reaction was make face as: What?... When started to talkme all her issues. Was amazin by me all her words. In first place said me that, since so much time ago, she take a psychiatric drug because has a mental disordier.

-Do you has a Metal Disordier?

-Yes, (she answerme)

-But how?

-In my fourteen years old, had a problem with my studys. Ever was good as student, but one day on my excercice class the teacher qualifyme very bad ussualy my notes was 10 o 9 (A or B) but now giveme a 5 (f).

-Ok, I understeand you but what was the issue?

-Oh this day feel not good. (woman say me with sadvoice).

Last, the woman explain me that her mother and she walked at one psychiatric institute because of she was not so good, had many feels verybad, indeed her own words were "I feel that the people, see me with bad eyes, as if they speak bad above me, all since my poor class note". Thanks toher word psychiatricman to did a interpretation which without any biological evidence.

From this day at woman beginn to take a psychiatric drug acording to Mental disordier in her personality. Today the woman has alot consecuences thanks at drug (she ist mechanicly slow, not thinking in short, her voice ist braking when spook, ist hard by she make good articulationships when move, indeed she to do reffer at her Head's left part ist nearly mismoved.) and maybe she never had anything, or a GUILT-FEEL Alone.

EUDIPICAL COMPLEX ESSAY PART ONE

Time ist to understood more above what ist symbologic answer to homosexual dream into man as twentyseven years old. As all psychoanalitic job his name not will be reveled because identity safe ist part of psychoanalize process. He'll be called alone T.J. that want to say "The jung". Before beggin with this case could be need what's happen into our social contex or into global context, so remember us at Psychoanalize ist science, somewhat even find explain the psychic reality and that maybe inside others cultures psychoanalize ist not good viewed, for this reason cloud be called "Social Resistance" fact which in another time'll get us great opportunity by speak about itself.

Now may I get readers at don't know what is psychoalalizes, please readable my passt text or search jobs from Sigmund Freud, Anna Freud, Melany Klein and more psychoanalize iconos, because they beginn this science and evolutioned this too. Now ist time to talk at pressent text enfold Classical psychoanalize and his evolutions but almust important ist take account at we are speech from psychoanalize into twentyone centurys, post modernism beyound, so called Psychoanalize New School.

T.J. ist a man that not understeand why had homosexual dream; when bring me his dreams the answere at I viewedable was that he get an Oral fix and Annal Fix, because of this are the erogen zones which him want to feel pleasure of course that is very natural to need pleasure on this zonebody. He want not stand with this answer only, Because enjoy his intrapsychic live he to feel big need about what represent this Dream and why was with a man and not with a woman.

This not was the first once that he and I speak us about himself, into anothers day had us fine opportunity by to get excelent convertation from all his live, and also not was the last. Now that he searched an aswere I said to he in fast: "Do you need know one thing in first place, well according with mental health science investigation, Homosexual personality don't are a mental disordier in the actual time thanks to "sexual politics" enforcementon the 20th Centurys between anothers things, But if a man or woman not understeand what happen with their sexuality it could become in mental disordier thanks to something so called Eudiphical complex unsolved, and not even Eudiphical complex become in mental disordier.

But, this are anothers stuffs, which maybe not will be need speak about this. How in passt convertations he xpresssed his Narcissist way of to get enviorenment conexion, at answer to his question been: "The fallus of your lover symbolism your father's fallous, but I'm reffering by your intrapsychic life: Whats is a father or what was a father by you, or what not was. In this way to bring all yourself by your father ist recognizer his "Authority" unconssiensously speanking, beacause of your are a man which to feel that get more importance than others; Indeed that so much others and could be trueth, but you need recognizer this feel of superiority all time with everybody, for it enjoy your sexual fantasy (ist called sexual fantasy not because nessesariously you want to realized it, maybe are incoussiensously, only) ist alone the way in how whole your pulsion energy reflex an imago about this man (making referrence of his saxual fanty and the sexual parthnership of them) that according with your Incounssiensouness is more than you; In thus form at anxiety envolvement in the narcicist personality enjoy yourself are slippage or reduced. In other words your neurosis of narciscims are laying for your sexual parthership, feeling in this way an authority and doing relief about anxiety because of your ego whatching the Reality aknowlagment that is

not better than everybody and you need feel someone better than
you or unless in the same possition.

ONE SOCIAL PERSONALITY

If you are interesed in this Chapter but not understeand or are not enfold into psychopathology studies, please don't to read pressent text, because of could be danger by your integrity or mental stability. Rather alone mental health professionals and futhure professionals able to read pressent Chapter.

Ist time for to do now awesome analyze about modern society and understand that each society get their own social personality and also this could be pathology or not, maybe pressent Chapter will be more efficient by men or women which studying societies, organizations and so on, of course by people that their goal-study ist to be human behaviors or to be human psyche, pressent text are excellent in strong previous knowledge.

Each social develop get different way of growth, so before to beginn ist well appoint that every psychoanalyze study envolving theories are based on investigationship by last be refforced within science method; in particular speaking about psychoanalyze case and in a lot others science forms all method ist spend by accomplished a law, findig ever universal law or one law as short as possible. For example into psychoanalize matter what ist the psychogenesys in psychopatology in first place.

Each culture get their owns rituals or traditions, So the science teaching us in how uncounsiensousness way this beginn. Some good example ist Oedipus complex and Incestuous traditions that many cultures got in the passt. Now when we are talking in how ist developed both every social personality and the called "Social Pathology" term that into another Chapter will seek more and may will get us great investigationship about them.

In the moment when ist spend "Social Personality" this don't want to say that the social context will be in this way forever, of course not, in the same form at "To be Human Personality" can become in another in the same manner "Social Personlaity" become in another according with laws our environment changes. This envioerement change coming soon will get the name from "Possitive Refforsment" and "Negative Refforsment" terms at in otherness time'll clear because of <<Psychoanalyze New School >> take both concepts but also take "Unconsiensouss Collective" concept.

However, knowing the psychoanalyze science this bring us an conceoptionship above to be human ist determined thanks to his or her environment, in other words, to be human take inside his/her owns personal and social develop a biology effect but in fist place pressent develop don't avoid how to be human stand determined for social context or environment not hi/her biology condition. Understanding awesome for example how "Sexual Politic" determined the sexuality in big part by political effect, or how the pathological mother wishes seek her son as object-sickness doing an transference enjoy false imago that she get about her son or Gosth-Son and more idealizations at could be pathological or not.

All writted in last lines stand in one hand but in the another hand able us to seek how "Social Personality" sometimes ist pathology sometime not. For example in one of my travels which got, will speak of three travels inside this same country, rather was possible to view how in differents states enjoy the same country the people take different personalyties, in other words how every state get different personalitys according each state; with this analyze get us almost questions for to do, by make conssiensouss what relationship get the laws that each state have. The next description of this "Social personality" not get nothing for to show in make offence by people or states anyway, envolving with it alone the knowledge about how personality ist developed. Somewhat will understand more from this issue or study object.

The three personality ways were "Obssesive Compulsive (toc)", "Narcissist" and "Obessesive Compulsive (tpoc)", where the citizens to share equals features into their interationship and conexion with anothers men or women over their owns environment, of course I able not to bring what cities were where this personality ways were detected. So to here almust ist need of remark.

But how could to view a better society or health society, but what ist a helath society or good society in the same form that individual develop, a social develop need accomplished cognitivegrowth, poverty ending, economy develop and so on giving it as health society concept, all that bring better opportunityes by their owns citizens. What want to say with this words or questions? easy with the context that to be human don't ist determined for our biology, rather ist determined for our social context and each social context bring in big part different feature of personalies ways.

If do you know more of "Social Patology" or what ist social pathology remind to read "Social Pathology".

SUICIDE BARRIER

Currently when to do my literature ever am thinking over many stuffs, because of in first place to need bring the better literary text, not only for get more loud my Ego (that indeed pressent text will be more about how rebuild and strong the Ego in the first session therapy into psychonalytic vision) is for when someone ist reading me, they need get awesome understanding of what I want to say, In other words every latter need be so clear by to share a better message.

As inside many literary text of psychoanalytic studies ist normal don't to share at name about the people that stand on psychoanalytic session in this form able us to save their identity. This literary job talk from one woman with twenntysix years old. But before to beginn ist time to have almust somethings so clear, for example what big difference are whether psychoanalitic therapy form and another psychodinamic therapy form that is important in the way in how our take us Sigmund Freud Theories and become thier investigations and MentalHealth studies into new theorie enfold psychic life adapted by twentyone centurys.

Psychoanalytic Therapy form could to bring better support by the psychic life above to be Human because of if remember us this mentalheal studies way ist based on pleasure theory between others but anothers therapies take account psychodinamic process anlone, forgotting Edipical Theory, Libidinal Theory or Objetal Theory between another. Now if you're reading pressent literary text and sound something on your mind that ist unawere for you, perphas for don't be envoling over mentalhealth studies, or if when you are reading pressent text to feel inside you somekind, could be questios, cloud be doubt, could be conectionship between the woman that will be writter to here and so on, don't worry ist great idea solving our your feels and questions of this job together your therapyman or woman.

The woman will be called "G.", sometime people ist finding me later the published in out my House about my therapie, I get many tools by surfing the psychic life of this people. "G" Search me one weekend as Ten night O'clock she was into high Ethilic State, in this way when said me " Need speak with you" my first think about her Ethilic State was: "Will be easy enjoy into her psychic animic, for the unconssiensous moment that she ist living; but of course it thought was big wrong. Now cooming soon will know us why.

"G" searching me with intention of talking with me, She beginned to say me all her issues in her live, the sickness in her brother, her economic conflict issues with drugadiction too, the bad relationship with her mother and the loud conflict the relationship with her boyfriend. As into many other different people get issues ist hard and find problem solving could be so hard. When the man or woman get an Ego so loud could be easy to solve pressent issues but when the ego ist unloud Ego's death currently are the solution only. How she was living over drugadiction environment her way in how to win her wages was enfolding one live as drugadict.

She reffer that years ago that also lived over drugaduction spending each drug possible, and as many persons also got another problems ways. But now the difference that today are ist in first place at relationship with her boyfriend, that at same time ist when sale to she the drugs. "G" was sharing how was this boyfriend relationship, where "G" was object-pleasure of He (the boyfriend) enjoy pathological relationship because the libidinal transference was maskared with his ambivalence feel against she whether in one hand his unconsiensous hat against his mother tranfered over "G" but in other hand the love for this object because he can be with "G" but she ever comeback, for this reason love so much this object because it object ever will be with me when "Ego" want and if Am bad never will do anything (ist how at boyfriend ist thinking), "G" also was doing one transference viewing on he her gosthfather where My father ist bad but I need be good with my father for to be my father because I belive that my father will bring me protection and in fisrt place love. According with her description this relation could be called Sadomasochist relationship where his sadic behaviors are need by she because "G" need someone as object by transfer too her libidinal pulssion becomoming all in pathological love.

"G" Also speak me about few week ago had bad moment because one of her friends to did the suicid as way in how problem solving and she ist thinking in spend suicid by to end with all conflicts. Why her boyfriend relation was so bad, well in first place, great or in other words health relationship bring ever bring us Eros and bad relationship bring or go Thanathos forward.

Here ist very important stress that this toxical conexion between she and he become her psychic life in an "I" without any defensse, rather, "G" only not transfered her libidinal pulsion, to end with each defensse. Now the suicide thought come because "Ego" ("G") have not another object in the life where draft good transference one health object because to need go Eros towards, other sickness object will be Thanathos often door, - ist here where I want to do great Parenthesis by understand why psychoanalyze aren't philosophy: another studies as philosophy could suggest that the suicide ist another way of to be or rather, other way of "Self"; but psychoanalyze spend methodology by mentalhealt investigation, rebuild and ever protect the Ego.

Ist Unavoidable get from us a man or woman that ist living pressent issue else, their defensse mechanism ist absolubtly ending, and get whether options to find helping inside health object or to end with the ego (suicide).

Now how Relief one ego when was Slippage, could sound easy but are not, in first place take account what defensse mechanism could us strong in fast (because with "G" was only one session, never had a professional-document by bring full therapy process) in this way the Insight will gave consciousness for example "G" into her Ethilical state in short beginned to speech from all her issues, and was for Insight when understood that she not get to stand with her boyfriend that ist the principal Thanathos walk, of course in her drug environment this achieve goal ist blind or unseekable because of the libidinal pulssion ist transfered in bad object (the boyfriend maybe with unconscious behaviors) and not in health object feeling big pleasure that nearly killer to ego.

According with liness ago Idealization, Introyection, was the first mechanism defensse which borned again over this insight. But the better new was Repression Currently when to do my literature ever am thinking over many stuffs, because of in first place to need bring the better literary text, not only for get more loud my Ego (that indeed pressent text will be more about how rebuild and strong the Ego in the first session therapy into psychonalytic vision) is for when someone ist reading me, they need get awesome understanding of what I want to say, In other words every latter need be so clear by to share a better message. When the man or woman to end with suicide thought his or her face become. I don't get doubt that was good psychoanalytical job because of achieve intention at one and fiveteen hours of morning was successful.

WRONG'S THERAPY

Talking about develop personality or foster, currently think us for example in Family environment. Enfolding psychoanalyze theories to be Human ist determined within social environment not biological within as anothers authors suggest. If remember us a little Sigmund Freud to share his theory with biological vision as Professional and Darwinist Influence, in other words perhaps Sigmund Freud was one man involved into big Global Revolution for his knowledge about Mentalhealth studies and investigation, but remember us that only not get us pressent man into Mentalhealth studies and investigations theories whichever suggest as Michel Foucault, Erick Ericksson, Donald Winnicott and more.

Likewish this literature as each literary job story across bring us opportunity by better to be Human growth because thinking a little and remind else, Psychoanalyze born enjoy Humanity vision if the world, ending with perverse To be Human Studies and xperiments that unfortunately today stand working yet. But thus lines don't are by talk about many ways of mishuman xperiment, but with at Humanity vision that Psychonalyze enfold, Will be almust clear if to share next experience.

First, before to speech of this new theory, will want suggest you great book entitled "Sólo Vine a Hablar por Teléfono" from Latinwritter Literature Nobel Prize winner called Gabriel Garcia Marquez. His book ist big criticism by Actual Psychiatric System where The people spend all their time and economy in something than never was trueth, also ist tremendous criticism in how Social sytem when determined To be Human Personality and not the Biology, Rather, could understeand that biology get little percent and Social Enviroment take other big part or big percent into to be human foster and personality develop.

However with this introduction ist time to seek another story with intentionship of Take more knowledge and to feel what's feeling our case into consult or Psychoanalytic process. Asgard ist the name in how will be called our young. Asgard is Mentalhealth student in a particular university in state to him. He begginned to take impression that someone ist ever back to him, as following to he. And in shorttime was to talk with his University Mentors. Called cellphone within psychopathologycal miss to him and never got an answer, also searched his Master woman for to share whole ist living, of course that never to said according with Asgard what been issues supply. But is clear at his Masterwoman never questioned him about this matter, in time when Asgard said all of people back him since time ago the Miss answer him saying: "I believe at you're Paranoid" an answer so offencive by him.

Could to suggest that before to say something to our coustumer our patients for example ever ist get on mind that our job ist understead to they. Enfold Disordier Stadistic Manuals and otherness of Dx, seem us that Asgard could to get Paranoid Disordier but this never been real, Why? easy he made many pics and save all email where enjoy others states into this same time his privasity been perturbed and each pic was evidence that of course some persons been back he.

As well as nessesariouly ist don't to do thus mistakes ways and remind Sigmund Freud (Modern Psychiatry Father) Prhase "All Psychology ist Social Psychology" in other words each society and environments get their own HealthCare concept (but among the science ist so easy get a Quantitative answer). On this Psychoanalytic Literature or Scientific Investigation seem us that Asgard real story and Gabriel Garcia Marquez book has big relationship, in first place over actual psychiatric system criticism.

For example the woman in Gabriel Garcia Marquez Book lived terrible issues about Schizophrenia Hallucinations among, that never been real, the whole book suggest perverse conspiration against she by to win great economic reward and bring false answer until the husband Saying "Your wife get many Mental Disorders, but don't worry we can help to she". In others words as xpert people ist Psychiatric institute how have the "reason". Her Husband gave us impression of Ignoranceman.

The woman and Asgard not got the same luck, Woman was declared among madness and Asgard never speaketh with anybody of how been all this issue, or how beggineth it, but spended thus strategy about pics and to save all evidence by unallow that someone will say that he has some Mental Disorder. Now in other tittles writheth time ago I suggest how ist so Dangerous seek Psychoanalyze as Philosophy because not are, Each people at believe Psychoanalyze as Philosophy ist ending with the whole objectivity whichever be «Ego Protect» or «Mind Healing», rather, Psychoanalyze ist to be human relief ever. By that Proof on patients showing aid them.

Pressent text should be an Introduction by otherness literary job and psychiatric investment above Prissions and Psychiatric Institutes.

EUDIPICAL COMPLEX SOLVED PART TWO

Later of some hours into psychoanalyzes process T.J. did consiensousness his unconsiensous insestous-desire torwards his Father or regardless towards one gosth-Father, in others words one father idealized in the psyche of T.J. this answerer us Why his sexual fantasy enfold even an Homosexual relationship with men which have more years old than him. T.J. told me about how nigths ago sleeping deeply for whole workforce spened under many time in the week making taks in his job and his Home, else. The appoint above pressent conversation been than this nigth Used his pans which He wears down him kneefs, At anxiety for don't understeand why had those behaviors were the fact for inquire me, What represent the form of sleeping? Currently our body to need fulment Regard enfolding each develop's zone in whole body on to be Human, had the better answer. In fast, explain to him too that: when was sleeping, to use his pans down for have a great dream, and how the body of himself unscociensouly whant to solve sexual fix or fixation, and how pressent fix are envolved into another behaviors over the life of him, also how thus behaviors sometime are pathologycal and sometime are not.

The face of "T.J.'' leave in fast when My answer is crossing His ears, -What happen?, the question born because of seem that could be better never before knew Wath repressent at way of sleeping days ago. -Don't worry! was the form in how become at conversation and in this way explain to him that, His libidinal energy Need to be spended on different activities or exercises, for example in therapy. But when it named libidinal pulsion ist many, could start a psychosomathic answer for have not a great meaning over this sexual pulsion or libidinal instict.

A little laught was possible to seek in time that "T.J." is hearing how are useable every moment about the libidinal pulsion of him. In fast, my next comment was setting one appointment enjoy the understeanding of "T.J." doing refference specialy that, his issues for unmake awesome or may unsatisfactory his anal-need in the toilet are product of spend the withholding and don't have largest awere of the matter in the form how heself psydinamic stand getting other reality on incounssiensous form. Where withholding represent at relationship between his parental figure or advisor, itself relations is well for gathering some fixes into annal-withholding evertaking different sexual life's, set up To be Human, in this time of "T.J" Personality.

In my mind been the idea that his "Puppets" could be inconssiessouly an object-love, and the anathomy or body of him get one prefference for to use the withholding itself which is spended also during all His life, as for example stress situation, picked parthnerlove, hobbies, favorit artist, at color by draw his bedroom again between other somethings.

As fast as possible "T.J," bring other questions, inquiring me Why day ago, indeed, days before at night sleeping within his Pans below, the Masturbation begun to be one daily excerce in every morning. Ask me else What happen if not solved the anal-fix. Latter of some hours of Analyzes teached to "T.J." explain him: how the sexual pulsions sometime are fixed in one sexual live-set develop in the Human Being growing and How when the Fixation ist solved put the Libido toward other zone of body where at Sexual pulsion or Energy (named energy for others authors as Donald Winnicot) could or not geting one Fixation. In others words, when his anal-fix in the will are solved, more zones from T.J.'s body may'll beginn to have at Need of solving his Regards. And How this are too, the way of answer Why masturbatorian behaviors on morning is a sadic excercise, Where

He's try, using his owns Phallos, of Solving the need from pleasure or regads how itself is Fixed on at Annos that pressent Yung have. Solving in this way every of whole feeling for want to Find pleasure whitin his Annus. Also his desires for destroy and killer whether animic or unanimic object enfolment in solving over anal fixation prosses. This behaviors sometime appeal other To Be Humans and currently the form of Destroy them is on the psychic's life althought other once in the Reality. Indeed tanathos drivers perphars could be Against himself in other form whom suicide and beyound.

Wheither annal and phallic fixes ever are envolved on otherness drivers as for example bad relationship with the father or mother'd be also into the parthnerlover, or more objets animed or unanimed and of course covered into whole personality features and skills, thus sometime are pathological or sad and sometime are not.

In other time of Psychoanalitic prosses latter of he to have an awere regard with the heself psychoanalitiy studies, "T.J." to share how other night long time afther spended an jersey as if be an Skirt and to feel need of seem his or imagen as a woman and at masturbation on morning not could over beggining even last it excerce, some sexual fantasy engagment relationship with others men and him need to get an answer about why been pressent fantasy and if the fixes are linked to this Sexual Fantasy in the one hand, but in the other hand was others ask in how heself to need problem solving in have a new girlfriend and the question been if whole this fixes are chained on (explain with my words) picked succesful an girlfriend or Delay this.

Latter of him told me how was all about need of pleasure when spended his Jersy by to feels himself as woman, my next answer as fast as shared was that (because of an insight could to be very slow and for another he is miswhatsover in so deep analityc process) the unsatisfactoriouly or Delayed try for have a new relationship been envolved in more fantasies and idealization about what woman he want as object love in this form idealizing a perfect animaded object love (according meet his standars) using the Jersey by gap or represented an idealized girl where He is in the Fantasy an idealized object of love. Now at next ask wichever I did to "T.J" were if the Man in the Sexual fantasy was a parent, friend, artist or a ficcion man, He can to say me: " Were a boy that time ago been possible know, our relationship as friend was as short as, realy". When to lay he well can to say me if could to describe this boy, Was so easy See how each skill to did one match within Him own personality.

In fast, our analyzes appontishment in a mirrow, named friend (the man in the fantasy) an object where is solved his intentionship for to have a girlfriend and at same time solved the Transference beggun in see one mirrow Other object that in one moment was as Fantasy may never over or Satisfactoriouly finished, and how the Issues with at annal withholding cover in a driver of contain the need of pleasure unconciensouly was the answer in realy not want be sodomiced for his friend or the mirrow that is an imago above him, rather T.J under his Fantasy is him Friend (mirrow) and his mask of woman is an Imago of what him wish in a woman (his perfect woman to match a love relationship). As "T.J." gap a Narcicist Personaly only heself (the mirrow or friend object) can sodomicer his own body it represented for He again. In an Imago about idealized-girlfriend solving the natural transference in then relationship with the object named friend, also solving the try of have the new girlfriend at same time, meaning dreams and sexual fantasies. For it, how all is part of one psychic-reality eachmore to need felt pleasure only not in the mind Also in the external reality thanks to it was in first place spend the Jersy as Skirt other object selection where the Jersey in the psychic of "T.J." an unanimic object-love called to the False girlfriend (because only exist on the fantasy but is represented for the clouthes, and the friend an ambibalince feels for him father solving his neurosis wich Narcicist personality appeal in his life and he don't migth sodomicer his father because is his father. To end He is both is father or authority represented for an friend where introyection take a palce and heself sodomicing or displasment his trancerence until an object love and at sdame time solving his Narcisist issues). In other words Friend spill himself than are at Father at same time sodomising him clothed woman wix Repressent Woman he wish like girlfriend throw Distortion Represention's Reality (adream).

EUDIPICAL COMPLEX SOLVED PART THREE

(Summer/2018).

Aslongeside from at lastest T.J's Therapy seasions day, He told me that all above therapy been talked in an friend conversation. An afther other time whole in the Neiborghood were awere of all detail. In fast, ask to him what was the trhouble when these. And Say me: "Just now, am feel that all ist Diferentship". Mein great sort anwerness suggest to him saying. - Talk alone, such of this been the words wich my psychoanalist investment about my mean, last some time from therapy "The Fantazied object picked for Delay the Sadic Behavihors aginst myself an ambivalent felth between Personality and authority So the very important is live the Here and Now". Because of you Nowhere haven't Homosexual Behaviors this are your present. (I end to say him).

So much time from adresse therapie day within "T.J." came to Divan (or coach) him into speech me what while he was Dreaming might to have a Remind when Many time ago in their Teenages Him and His brother meet other boy was to look pornografy to the Internet how all his friends does. He did clear than in those time His Sexual desire were very Low and make know how when standing on Internet with his Friend and Brother, the Friend sugget to his Brother to Show Homosexual pornografy but Him Brother appeal in fast saying hat not will Seen this because is not over their Wells.

Latter Him confes me that his Sexual Fantacies no were only in a Dream how the Firsth Day of Analyzes spaek me. Indeed got some relationship and surffer others Facts how in the Pornografy. When Him post to mein knowlagde this the next Question was If before of the Moment in that Him, His brother and his Friend goes to Internet to look pornografy He saw pornografy before or been the First moment wich get this xperience? Why He Feel about his friend for sugget the Homosexual pornografy?

Each words were sinseriouly when say me: No, me never think in look this screen because by our Education that our family bring is Bad, this was the firsth time in to be meet Pornografy kinds, and Saith me too; As the friend from my brother and me even got him over the people with better qualifys in whole asignature, Me not feel nothing bad agaisnt Him. But the Reasson was in my Brother. At next atachment to he for my part was in the very good for speak me it reprimed. Because gave us more light about his Sexual Fantasy and desire for look pornografy. So His relaxing been in time at answer Him, appontisment in His wishes for Seen this pornografy category was because an External Object called Friend to teach by him Learn what Category from Sexual Imagen should to See, and Unconsienssouly a desire for to get an Example taked, what the Object Idealied as best option to Seek Sexual Imagens, Here the reason in how you learned to choose Sexual Imagens by to upon pleasure.

Afther to hear whole He Told me that never thinked in how one moment exchange all alive. In the other hand suggest them that exchange from category slowly is alright to stop this desire becuase as learned what is the form in to get Sexual Relationship for some imagens or pornografie only to need learn what way of Sexuality wish across imagens is teached and in real life too, because of psychoanalizes solving him past by living nowhere. So in way at him mind get more xperience wich him wish his unconciensous will remeber more imagen in wether from imagen and in real life.

Howover at though, migth don't bring to "T.J." all Analyzed into Session as for example that him future fantasies will reflex such wishes insolved into distorcioned way. The wish under Libidinal pulsion as biological Human Being fact will drafting one imaginary-object in a dream currently bizzar.

EUDIPICAL COMPLEX SOLVED PART FOUR

(Augtun/2018)

Adressen T.J psychoanalizes time, one day comeback to me talken me than Him is wreitch for begun a Live where is good get Learning wich could to arrave him over Great Sexual activity with beautuful women at he will start new Learning, spending other pleasure supply just as Straight pornofigrafy, and tryning meet some women while marrier. Soon my fees words shared to him was at if in a time him feel something Direfent wich don't upon at Sexual Clima are because over our brain have something called Neuro-transmisors and thise make synaptical conexion in time that is Learned something, In other words when new kinds enhance our Encephalic System feel start to work making conexion between some neuro transmisor meet other neurotransmisors. For example when his reception above fisrtime of looking pornografy, when his brother and friend stand with he, his neurotrasmition was doing many jobs aknowlagment at reality that ist how One imago called Friend an Idealized object (Idealized Object becase he the Friend ever had taskwood on School, same than T.J. in there time wished) teached him "The Bliss" but too Neourotransmisors did him Synaptical job when he looks his Brother and Remembering whole relationship with He enfolding Anbivalence feeling (above his brother and solving what his brother want or what him friend gonn) wich inconciensouly T.J. have, because of all people in the world have thise. Rether, Synaptical conexions Should start from the beggin or bleam new conexions; in at same way if He Learn New lenguage Synapses will does conection, but if not practice or spend the Lenguage shrewd will forgot in bigest part or nearly absolubtly this, in at same way When try to learn other something in the begining Synaptical conection not strength so much At new driver, behavior or Personality Skill itself should be refforce everytime by Neouro Transmisors make strongly synaptical job or disappear. In other words he shouldn't loom for the fast answer because anyone learn to Speak in one month, or to be good drumer in the first experience So if want to be a drumer could to felt different Styles perhaps every Style like that, perhaps dislike.

In at same way if him Across his live get or got otherness experiences wichen today like not to do once again, should him learn what he's desaring because of whole need of pleasure enfold him willing Plot in his external objects, transfering such Psychic Energy or called to Biological impulse where itself shall to be delay damping, choosen lots objects in the one hand, and in the other Hand itself Libidinal pulsion or Biological instict or Psychic Energy will choose one object acording with his experience of live, for example when Teenager him had learned whom cloud lowing his Psychic Energy (unconsiensously) doing refecence in his first nearly Sexual xpericnce that someone (friend) teached him what is better. Now his Synaptical conection need get other xperecience and learnings by the future chosee other objects where tranfece his Libidinal instit and All that's hold thise.

SOCIAL SPLINTER STILL PERSONALITYS

Today into 21 Centurys ad world is another astrological, metaphysical, scientificly, socialy; kingdoms araise strongly and more soon, challenges overwhileeng in the daily of each people. As in the earlier talk you, the Enteral World puts greastes diferent lookings, this and more of the wrote under Chapter Social context were Social Hitos that the Globe took Testhify. In then pressent time wichen Psychoanalizes strongment, leap our vision in the 'stoods from lot's of things. Come from the Several Setting because of Freedom's Thinkers, was at the vision in what Sigmund Freud Gather His theorys and his unrebutables. Itself is named Social Determination.

Sigmund Freud step clearly who is Human Being social Determined and not Biological determined. At same trouble that others afther Him called "Antipsychiatric Movement", in that They else were sticking than Psychiatric catchs ad wrong of look to the people Determied by the Biological Facts. In so, could us rename to the Doctor Sigmund Freud the first anti-psychiatric, an Entiltment in worthy any shortly. But not were Him only when bring to know those to the people, academics, and other meaners in the Context too. Therefore He forecast Human Being Thought because of His topics and otherwise. In ad Same Way most took His fashon's: Melany Klein, Alfred Adler, Otto Rank, Donald Winnicot, Ana Freud, Michel Focult and to do so. Them alone not were Seeked what's Freud teach, Their social contributions cheaped our Today's world. In personal point opinion scratchs If one day someone ask me what other bigger contribution still the Psychoanalizes or modern psychiatric? Are at willing reject aroundig 70's Decadetes in then Scietific job by the wheel in-put wich is: Louding Freud's work in how Social facts, only not Natural Social process facts is manipuled consiensously and incounsiensouly to the Human Being.

To speech more to the matter, Psychoanalizes into the 21 Century flip Up other Interesant case in how A man Tell us how Is visited to the Political liberal Party to offer something, by He would to exchange heself own thinkig. -Shrewd this are an Even not reveled Names Because our Professional psychoanalitic Investment-. Him plot that in an Inverview He were psychoanalized and last fractal time of the well psychoanalizes wich succesfuly, in fast, Afther were psychoanalized LPP (liberal political party) find out Him too propose gifts; Gifts how He could uptown If twice Him personality for another again. Personality than shall to wears Sexual orientation away, inclunding Homosexual Thrivers; leaveing than those 'd to do Him actual sexual orientation over Bisexuality Bahaviors. All wrote ago answer us tidy that Psychoanalyzers pin out in Ad 70's Decadetes, How External -from the "I or ego"- Socials facts (superego) "screw" enhancing than Homosexuality should stand off from the Disordier Stadistic Manual; to it in those way be part forth the Favoritism in the pop of Political campings.

Whenever to migth wet at Psychoanalitic job and whom itself according meet Freud and otherwise Human Being is Dertermined because of social facts, Are need strongly remark than now as in whole case not will be Reveled at names from people sorrounding this pressent situation wich "MAM" (is how will tell us our psychoanalized) puts into March 2019 were in His Church were visited by the Democratic Political party from the United States (again ist feed to say than at Name from the representative from the party not will be reveled). "MAM" describe in How his poll into Global political means are so loudly had two ways of thinking around Political and Social Step in at secound Decadete Just latter of begging ad 21 Century.

Wether are chained in at Building Wall than USA in then same time or period of time that's writing press Scientific hub and when him were arrived in at wheel visited.

The frist Thought in the one hand come on when lot of people suggest than mentioned Wall was begun because of Several and Horrific Terror Attaks amongst United States Citizens, for that Donald Trump as President of Thise Country upset the country could to craft at Wall in South Border to draft save and care by his citizens, because ist at place where this Criminals bunch, inner to the Nation. So in the other hand the Secunth Thought fix new United States Wall because somebody seem than thise were started and early performed forth Social mainers wich wishn't anymore or deny such homosexual behaviors inner at Homelanders (something absurd to "MAM" who His tolk to me on Free Asociation) holding Him testify went to make claer than at Secunth point of view Were why Liberal Party catch meet Him; because "MAM" over his poll got much success. So if he forecast again His Personality features as in the past before his Psychoanalizes simpatizers with that Party could worship to He on Different ways.

In the Row in what "MAM" Lived, him explain clarely his Clash around Political Liberal Party from the United States and them Ideology folding some simpatizer wich aren't part from at Party but shrewd promove proundly them Social Ideology or Draws. In fast, "MAM" speak me his Grief in say to the Liberal party Representatives and otherwise ad not will become him Personality Stills appontishment over him Sexuality. But neither, who He gets his own vision of the World, could aid wet Deny Political intention in some Business or Kinds and not forecast his Sexual insigths again.

Nevertheless Today I don't know if "MAM" were part from the achievements than his supricers got. I only am awere in him not leave his Personality hence more. Whenever Pressent case screen us loudly just what Psychoanalizes under twentyone Century puts ad at same kind that in to 70's Decades psychoanalizt as Michel Foucult and otherness grasp on them Scientific Investment above the psyhiatric power and how political partys might Spend Thise in to have influence and followers. Overviewing what realy was at reason in that Homosexuality were off from the Mental Dosordier Stadistic, rather that politicals step at buch in gets most sympatizers offering Sexual freedom, setting what we are talking in stand off from the DSM.

The whole earlier told about at fight wichen Psychoanalizes has against Biological Determination, same thinking provideless at the folks leave them personalitys in many case. So pick up the point over who social facts is when Realy are Determing at Human Being down political conspires, social contexts, Family cyrcle, Social growth, Social evelopment and other Human Relationship. However I'm not searching end meet Homosexuality behaviors on anyone (watching wretch just as folks wet this psychodinamic way could to has succes development without anahnce anyother pathology), but stick Biological Determination of To be Human is Deceive alone.

REGARDS

Glued at my brach jump on like gottaness by widespread to the readers from dis Scientific Investigation as literacy gender What has in my personal and profesional wax. Shrwed draw from thus, wich must noted shortly, my life couldn't be at same because of his or her teaching ever was at better on me, fluxing as well mein cognositive growth since my teenyearhood until today worlds. To ending this scientific work (hoping at next writing due) are very important aknowlegment To be human never must be any kind if not were for other Human being, We as mankind alive on a world where someone insteand in the arms from otters by vex less and flowrish thogether. On First place before anyone my big and deeply thanksful is by my teacher form High School the Miss director woman of "Fernando of Tapia" Institutes an School in at State myself born, she is called Basilia is whole I can rimeid above her. I was her Literacy learner, Might remeber yet at time in hers classmate. Been she a Old very old woman were exemplar one by me because the Fundation from hers own School been woman looking that in at time she were jung at education by Women rewardless on this country was as far as more than by the men. When older she getting must than seventy years old is hinting few Universitys on set up by Learners Philosophy, Spain, English, Logic and other matters. Basilia is by me someone wich ever must remember for being she hux foster me by beging University Studies, at education and Love for teaching wears her in at Soul by me were a Sun than expect many from students waiting at better from themselves. Her blue eyes lihgting yelled Shakesperean poes must be on me always.

As well as granting of hearlty reckognet, wanna dedicate this Scientific Work by Maru Eugenie Chavez at Miss from Psychopatology and Otter Forensic matters I got on University. She were even funny. At manner of learning inner in that classmate surface from seriousness to the wityness. Meet her got the naive in going to a lot of consultants grasping children, olders, yungers and so on. I thought at lasty classroom wich were with her perhaps was at better great class from Intelectual ones yielding at psychogenesis from Mental pathologys off-course I learned too from my parthers of that classmate but like credit is by This woman our Passion for Sigmund Freud and the old Psychoanalitic world and in the post modernizm followers was what doesn't never outsatand on School every minute on such Classing were very important and shwred interesant. In at Same way otterwise hux are granted with my rewards is at Prof. Arturo Montez otter fashon from psychoanalitics under University I belive thy both were wich harvest on me Psychoanalitic sow, nevertheless most that practice or consultans in at same bunch did mit maru the Preaching paths, Arturo Montez draws into Mental illnes were most theoric booking every week many reading that sometimes could be wacko read that but needy by our wheel.

In the Oder hand got other teacher and miss But don't remind so good what her or his name is, so than Got up a Miss from PsychoEducation were explored Ikons like Jonh Look, Baruch Spinoza, William James and other soon. And to end an Special Regards to Theresa Leal at miss than thogether craft up a Psychometrics hint than can uptown in other from mein milestones as well.

REFFERENCE

*64 1856-1939, F. S. (2013). Group psychology and the analysis of the ego. Place of publication not identified: Hardpress Ltd.

*12 Accountability in Governance. (n.d.). Retrieved May 02, 2019, from https://siteresources.worldbank.org/PUBLICSECTORANDGOVERNANCE/Resources/AccountabilityGovernance.pdf.

*29 American Psychiatric Association: Diagnostic and Statistical Manual of Mental Disorders, Fifth Edition. Arlington, VA, American Psychiatric Association, 2013.

*39 AHMED, A. (2019, May 8). Instead of a Border Wall, Some Scientists Want Clean Energy. Retrieved September 28, 2019, from https://www.theatlantic.com/science/archive/2019/05/instead-border-wall-some-scientists-want-clean-energy/588886/

*21 (n.d.). BibleGateway. Retrieved from https://www.biblegateway.com/passage/?search=Matthew+17&version=NIV

*10 Britannica, T. E. (2018, July 23). Islamic State in Iraq and the Levant. Retrieved April 05, 2019, from https://www.britannica.com/topic/Islamic-State-in-Iraq-and-the-Levant

*41 Booth, R. (2017, November 26). The killing of Osama bin Laden: how the White House changed its story. Retrieved September 29, 2019, from https://www.theguardian.com/world/2011/may/04/osama-bin-laden-killing-us-story-change

*20 Bowman, E., & Martin, M. (2019, March 24). With The Collapse Of The ISIS 'Caliphate,' A Camera Lens Lingers On Those Left Behind. Retrieved from https://www.southcarolinapublicradio.org/post/collapse-isis-caliphate-camera-lens-lingers-those-left-behind

*6 Bump, P. (2018, December 11). Trump's arguments for necessity of border wall have already been broadly debunked. Retrieved March 04, 2019, from https://www.washingtonpost.com/politics/2018/12/11/trumps-arguments-necessity-border-wall-have-already-been-broadly-debunked/?noredirect=on&utm_term=.dc60a86ad0d9

*46 Bram, L. L., Phillips, R. S., Dickey, N. H., Funk & Wagnalls, & Funk & Wagnalls Staff. (1983). Funk and Wagnalls New Encyclopedia. In N. Encyclopedia (Ed.), Freud. Sigmund (pp. 82–84). Pan-American Republics and United States: Funk & Wagnalls.

*3 Brief History of the Mexican Peso and its devaluation against the US dollar. (n.d.). Retrieved March 03, 2019, from http://en.nadglobal.com/blog/brief-history-of-the-mexican-peso-and-its-devaluation-against-the-us-dollar

*58 Britannica, T. E. of E. (2019, September 10). Seppuku. Retrieved October 12, 2019, from https://www.britannica.com/topic/seppuku

*47 Cherry, K. (2019, June 24). What Are Freud's Stages of Psychosexual Development? Retrieved September 29, 2019, from https://www.verywellmind.com/freuds-stages-of-psychosexual-development-2795962

*35 Convention against Torture. (n.d.). Retrieved September 28, 2019, from https://www.ohchr.org/en/professionalinterest/pages/cat.aspx.

*24 Comitee, I. R. (Ed.). (n.d.). Refugee crisis. Retrieved from https://www.rescue.org/topic/refugee-crisis

*25 Comitee, I. R. (n.d.). Venezuela. Retrieved from https://www.rescue.org/country/venezuela

*61 Death Instint Thanatos. (2019). Retrieved October 12, 2019, from https://www.encyclopedia.com/medicine/psychology/psychology-and-psychiatry/death-instinct.

*22 Diagnostic and Statistical Manual of Mental Disorders, Fifth Edition. Arlington, VA, American Psychiatric Association, 2013.

*16 Diaz, K. (2018, February 05). Designer of solar border wall threatens to sue Trump for taking his idea. Retrieved May 13, 2019, from https://www.chron.com/news/politics/article/Designer-of-solar-border-wall-threatens-to-sue-12553107.php

*51 Discrimination | psychology. (n.d.). Retrieved September 29, 2019, from https://www.britannica.com/science/discrimination-psychology

*26 Facing an Unprecedented Migration Crisis in Latin America and the Caribbean. (2019, March 29). Retrieved from https://www.worldbank.org/en/news/opinion/2019/03/29/america-latina-y-el-caribe-frente-a-una-crisis-migratoria-sin-precedentes

*40 In the press - "Conspiracy theories thrive on lack of proof." (2011, May 3). Retrieved September 29, 2019, from https://www.france24.com/en/20110503-osama-bin-laden-conspiracy-theories-thrive-on-lack-of-proof-obama-war-terror-photographs

*17 Islamic State group defeated as final territory lost, US-backed forces say. (2019, March 23). Retrieved May 14, 2019, from https://www.bbc.com/news/world-middle-east-47678157

*11 Ivan.restrepo. (n.d.). United Nations Office on Drugs and Crime. Retrieved April 30, 2019, from https://www.unodc.org/unodc/en/treaties/single-convention.html

*5 Exchange-Rates.org world currency exchange rates and currency exchange rate history. (n.d.). Retrieved March 04, 2019, from https://www.exchange-rates.org/currentRates/A/USD

*36 Garcia, M. J. (2009, January 26). Convention Against Torture [Dataset]. Retrieved September 28, 2019, from https://fas.org/sgp/crs/intel/RL32438.pdf

*48 Gaur, A., & Young, G. (1998, June 20). Telepathy | psychology. Retrieved September 29, 2019, from https://www.britannica.com/topic/telepathy

*7 Gilsinan, K. (2018, December 11). Trump Keeps Invoking Terrorism to Get His Border Wall. Retrieved March 04, 2019, from https://www.theatlantic.com/international/archive/2018/12/trump-incorrectly-links-immigration-terrorism/576358/

*23 Guilfoyle, K. (2019, September 13). In Venezuela, America Is the Beacon of Hope for a Struggling Nation. Retrieved from https://townhall.com/columnists/kimberlyguilfoyle/2019/09/13/in-venezuela-america-is-the-beacon-of-hope-for-a-struggling-nation-n2553029?amp=true&__twitter_impression=true

*59 Hara-kiri. (n.d.). Retrieved October 12, 2019, from https://www.dictionary.com/browse/hara-kiri.
*8 Jansen, B. (2018, December 06). DHS: Convicted murderer arrested for illegal entry as part of migrant caravan. Retrieved March 04, 2019, from https://www.usatoday.com/story/news/2018/11/30/dhs-murderer-gang-member-arrested-part-migrant-caravan/2163762002/

*49 Kalsang Bhutia, T. K. B., Lotha, G., Rogers, K., & Young, G. (1998, July 20). psychokinesis | Definition & Experimental Results. Retrieved September 29, 2019, from https://www.britannica.com/topic/psychokinesis

*57 International Feedom Religion, U. S. C. on. (n.d.). Welcome to USCIRF. Retrieved October 12, 2019, from https://www.uscirf.gov/.

*19 Kelly, G. (11 de enero de 2017). ¿Puedes distinguir los tweets reales de Donald Trump de las falsificaciones de MSM? Toma nuestro test para averiguarlo. Recuperado de https://www.telegraph.co.uk/men/the-filter/can-tell-real-donald-trump-tweets-msm-fakes-take-quiz-find/

*63 Life Instinct. (2019). Retrieved October 12, 2019, from https://www.encyclopedia.com/psychology/dictionaries-thesauruses-pictures-and-press-releases/life-instinct-eros

*33 Lotha, G., Sampaolo, M., Techs, N., & Zeidan, A. (2014, October 1). Islamic State in Iraq and the Levant | History & Facts. Retrieved September 26, 2019, from https://www.britannica.com/topic/Islamic-State-in-Iraq-and-the-Levant

*34 Lotha, G., Sampaolo, M., Techs, N., & Zeidam, A. (2014b, October 1). Islamic State in Iraq and the Levant - Expansion and declaration of a caliphate. Retrieved September 26, 2019, from https://www.britannica.com/topic/Islamic-State-in-Iraq-and-the-Levant/Expansion-and-declaration-of-a-caliphate

*15 Orr, G., Hesson, T., Choi, M., & Orr, G. (2019, January 09). From 'wall' to 'barrier': How Trump's vision for the border keeps changing. Retrieved May 13, 2019, from https://www.politico.com/story/2019/01/08/trumps-vision-wall-concrete-steel-changes-1088714

*52 Tanenhaus, S. (2018, October 11). How Trumpism Will Outlast Trump. Retrieved October 9, 2019, from https://time.com/magazine/us/5421567/october-22nd-2018-vol-192-no-16-u-s/.

*1 The Tequila crisis in 1994. (n.d.). Retrieved April 03, 2019, from https://economics.rabobank.com/publications/2013/september/the-tequila-crisis-in-1994/

*13 Trotsenburg, A. V. (2019, March 29). Facing an Unprecedented Migration Crisis in Latin America and the Caribbean. Retrieved May 05, 2019, from https://www.worldbank.org/en/news/opinion/2019/03/29/america-latina-y-el-caribe-frente-a-una-crisis-migratoria-sin-precedentes.

*14 Trump proposes solar panel wall for Mexican border. (2017, June 22). Retrieved May 13, 2019, from https://www.bbc.com/news/av/world-us-canada-40365031/trump-proposes-solar-panel-wall-for-mexican-border

*39 Lardner, R. (2011, September 28). U.S. tells court bin Laden photos must stay secret. Retrieved September 29, 2019, from https://www.salon.com/2011/09/28/us_bin_laden_photos/

*62 Life Instinct. (2019). Retrieved October 12, 2019, from https://www.encyclopedia.com/psychology/dictionaries-thesauruses-pictures-and-press-releases/life-instinct-eros

*50 Lotha, G., Rogers, K., & Sampaolo, M. (2019, June 23). Perceptual learning. Retrieved September 29, 2019, from https://www.britannica.com/topic/perceptual-learning

*53 Macro-Theory: Definition of Macro-Theory by Lexico. (n.d.). Retrieved October 12, 2019, from https://www.lexico.com/en/definition/macro-theory.

*2 Musacchio, & Aldo. (2012, July 13). Mexico's financial crisis of 1994-1995. Retrieved April 03, 2019, from https://dash.harvard.edu/handle/1/9056792

*38 Nations, U. (2019a). Asylum. In U. S. America (Ed.), Standard Language Addendum: Asylum, Withholding of Removal & Convention Against Torture (p. 2). America: United States.

*37 Nations, U. (2019b). Convention Against Torture. In U. S. America (Ed.), Standard Language Addendum: Asylum, Withholding of Removal. & Convention Against Torture (p. 9). America: United States.

*45 Sansal, P. (2019, June 18). Domesticating the Giant: The Global Governance of Migration. Retrieved September 29, 2019, from https://www.cfr.org/report/domesticating-giant-global-governance-migration

*54 Sociology Dictionary, O. E. (n.d.). macrosociology definition. Retrieved October 12, 2019, from https://sociologydictionary.org/macrosociology/.

*43 Swinford, S. (2011, May 5). Doubts grow on US version of strike against bin Laden. Retrieved September 29, 2019, from https://www.smh.com.au/world/doubts-grow-on-us-version-of-strike-against-bin-laden-20110505-1eaah.html

*42 Swinford, S., & Souza, P. (2011, May 4). Osama bin Laden dead: Blackout during raid on bin Laden compound. Retrieved September 29, 2019, from https://www.telegraph.co.uk/news/worldnews/al-qaeda/8493391/Osama-bin-Laden-dead-Blackout-during-raid-on-bin-Laden-compound.html

*4 UN, United Nations, UN Treaties, Treaties. (n.d.). Retrieved April 03, 2019, from https://treaties.un.org/pages/ViewDetails.aspx?src=TREATY&mtdsg_no=VI-15&chapter=6&clang=_en

*30 UNODC - Human Trafficking. (n.d.). Retrieved September 25, 2019, from https://www.unodc.org/unodc/en/human-trafficking/index.html

*27 Unodc.org. (2019). What is Human Trafficking?. [online] Available at: https://www.unodc.org/unodc/en/human-trafficking/what-is-human-trafficking.html [Accessed 23 Sep. 2019].

*9 U.S.-backed forces declare victory over ISIS in Syria. (2019, March 23). Retrieved April 05, 2019, from https://www.euronews.com/2019/03/23/u-s-backed-forces-declare-victory-over-isis-syria-n972401

*28 Van Trotsenburg, A. (2019). Facing an Unprecedented Migration Crisis in Latin America and the Caribbean. [online] World Bank. Available at: https://www.worldbank.org/en/news/opinion/2019/03/29/america-latina-y-el-caribe-frente-a-una-crisis-migratoria-sin-precedentes [Accessed 23 Sep. 2019].

*18 Wedeman, B., & Said-Moorhouse, L. (2019, March 23). ISIS has lost its final stronghold in Syria, the Syrian Democratic Forces says. Retrieved May 14, 2019, from https://edition.cnn.com/2019/03/23/middleeast/isis-caliphate-end-intl/index.html

*44 Wikipedia. (2019, September 24). conspiracy theories about when and how Osama bin Laden died. Retrieved September 29, 2019, from https://en.wikipedia.org/wiki/Osama_bin_Laden_death_conspiracy_theories

*31 What is Human Trafficking? (n.d.). Retrieved September 25, 2019, from https://www.unodc.org/unodc/en/human-trafficking/what-is-human-trafficking.html

*56 Worldwide Religious Persecution. (2018, November 6). Retrieved October 12, 2019, from https://www.nae.net/worldwide-religious-persecution/.

*32 Zeidan, A., Lotha, G., Young, G., Techs, N., Cunningham, J. M., Sinha, S., & Sampaulo, M. (2011, July 6). Syrian Civil War | Facts & Timeline. Retrieved September 26, 2019, from https://www.britannica.com/event/Syrian-Civil-War

BIBLIOGRAFIA

1856-1939, F. S. (2013). Group psychology and the analysis of the ego. Place of publication not identified: Hardpress Ltd.

A. (1994). Diagnostic and Stadistic Manual of Mental Disordiers DSM-IV. ISBN 8-89042-062-9

Accountability in Governance. (n.d.). Retrieved May 02, 2019, from https://siteresources.worldbank.org/PUBLICSECTORANDGOVERNANCE/Resources/AccountabilityGovernance.pdf.

American Psychiatric Association: Diagnostic and Statistical Manual of Mental Disorders, Fifth Edition. Arlington, VA, American Psychiatric Association, 2013.

AHMED, A. (2019, May 8). Instead of a Border Wall, Some Scientists Want Clean Energy. Retrieved September 28, 2019, from https://www.theatlantic.com/science/archive/2019/05/instead-border-wall-some-scientists-want-clean-energy/588886/

(n.d.). BibleGateway. Retrieved from https://www.biblegateway.com/passage/?search=Matthew+17&version=NIV

Bram, L. L., Phillips, R. S., Dickey, N. H., Funk & Wagnalls, & Funk & Wagnalls Staff. (1983). Funk and Wagnalls New Encyclopedia. In N. Encyclopedia (Ed.), Freud. Sigmund (pp. 82–84). Pan-American Republics and United States: Funk & Wagnalls.

Brief History of the Mexican Peso and its devaluation against the US dollar. (n.d.). Retrieved March 03, 2019, from http://en.nadglobal.com/blog/brief-history-of-the-mexican-peso-and-its-devaluation-against-the-us-dollar

Britannica, T. E. (2018, July 23). Islamic State in Iraq and the Levant. Retrieved April 05, 2019, from https://www.britannica.com/topic/Islamic-State-in-Iraq-and-the-Levant

Britannica, T. E. of E. (2019, September 10). Seppuku. Retrieved October 12, 2019, from https://www.britannica.com/topic/seppuku

Booth, R. (2017, November 26). The killing of Osama bin Laden: how the White House changed its story. Retrieved September 29, 2019, from https://www.theguardian.com/world/2011/may/04/osama-bin-laden-killing-us-story-change

Bowman, E., & Martin, M. (2019, March 24). With The Collapse Of The ISIS 'Caliphate,' A Camera Lens Lingers On Those Left Behind. Retrieved from https://www.southcarolinapublicradio.org/post/collapse-isis-caliphate-camera-lens-lingers-those-left-behind

Bump, P. (2018, December 11). Trump's arguments for necessity of border wall have already been broadly debunked. Retrieved March 04, 2019, from https://www.washingtonpost.com/politics/2018/12/11/trumps-arguments-necessity-border-wall-have-already-been-broadly-debunked/?noredirect=on&utm_term=.dc60a86ad0d9

Convention against Torture. (n.d.). Retrieved September 28, 2019, from https://www.ohchr.org/en/professionalinterest/pages/cat.aspx.

Craig, G. J., & Baucum, J. (1999). Human Develop. Pearson Education, Inc. ISBN 0-13-922774-1 translated in His 9th Edition 2009 down ISBN 978-607-442-310-5

Cherry, K. (2019, June 24). What Are Freud's Stages of Psychosexual Development? Retrieved September 29, 2019, from https://www.verywellmind.com/freuds-stages-of-psychosexual-development-2795962

Comitee, I. R. (Ed.). (n.d.). Refugee crisis. Retrieved from https://www.rescue.org/topic/refugee-crisis

Comitee, I. R. (n.d.). Venezuela. Retrieved from https://www.rescue.org/country/venezuela

Consil, S. (2019). Venezuelans Must Resolve Crisis Themselves, Security Council Delegates Agree while Differing over Legitimacy of Contending Parties | Meetings Coverage and Press Releases. [online] Un.org. Available at: https://www.un.org/press/en/2019/sc13719.doc.htm [Accessed 23 Sep. 2019].

Death Instint Thanatos. (2019). Retrieved October 12, 2019, from https://www.encyclopedia.com/medicine/psychology/psychology-and-psychiatry/death-instinct.

Diagnostic and Statistical Manual of Mental Disorders, Fifth Edition. Arlington, VA, American Psychiatric Association, 2013.

Diaz, K. (2018, February 05). Designer of solar border wall threatens to sue Trump for taking his idea. Retrieved May 13, 2019, from https://www.chron.com/news/politics/article/Designer-of-solar-border-wall-threatens-to-sue-12553107.php

Discrimination | psychology. (n.d.). Retrieved September 29, 2019, from https://www.britannica.com/science/discrimination-psychology

Exchange-Rates.org world currency exchange rates and currency exchange rate history. (n.d.). Retrieved March 04, 2019, from https://www.exchange-rates.org/currentRates/A/USD

Facing an Unprecedented Migration Crisis in Latin America and the Caribbean. (2019, March 29). Retrieved from https://www.worldbank.org/en/news/opinion/2019/03/29/america-latina-y-el-caribe-frente-a-una-crisis-migratoria-sin-precedentes

Fromm, E., & Maccoby, M. (2018). A Mexican Peasant Village. Social Character in a Mexican Village, 31-40. doi:10.4324/9781351306409-2

Garcia, M. J. (2009, January 26). Convention Against Torture [Dataset]. Retrieved September 28, 2019, from https://fas.org/sgp/crs/intel/RL32438.pdf

Gaur, A., & Young, G. (1998, June 20). Telepathy | psychology. Retrieved September 29, 2019, from https://www.britannica.com/topic/telepathy

Gilsinan, K. (2018, December 11). Trump Keeps Invoking Terrorism to Get His Border Wall. Retrieved March 04, 2019, from https://www.theatlantic.com/international/archive/2018/12/trump-incorrectly-links-immigration-terrorism/576358/

Glass, R. M. (2009). Diagnostic and Statistical Manual of Mental Disorders (DSM). AMA Manual of Style. doi:10.1093/jama/9780195176339.022.529

Guilfoyle, K. (2019, September 13). In Venezuela, America Is the Beacon of Hope for a Struggling Nation. Retrieved from https://townhall.com/columnists/kimberlyguilfoyle/2019/09/13/in-venezuela-america-is-the-beacon-of-hope-for-a-struggling-nation-n2553029?amp=true&__twitter_impression=true

Hara-kiri. (n.d.). Retrieved October 12, 2019, from https://www.dictionary.com/browse/hara-kiri.

Life Instinct. (2019). Retrieved October 12, 2019, from https://www.encyclopedia.com/psychology/dictionaries-thesauruses-pictures-and-press-releases/life-instinct-eros

In the press - "Conspiracy theories thrive on lack of proof." (2011, May 3). Retrieved September 29, 2019, from https://www.france24.com/en/20110503-osama-bin-laden-conspiracy-theories-thrive-on-lack-of-proof-obama-war-terror-photographs

International Feedom Religion, U. S. C. on. (n.d.). Welcome to USCIRF. Retrieved October 12, 2019, from https://www.uscirf.gov/.

Ivan.restrepo. (n.d.). United Nations Office on Drugs and Crime. Retrieved April 30, 2019, from https://www.unodc.org/unodc/en/treaties/single-convention.html

Jansen, B. (2018, December 06). DHS: Convicted murderer arrested for illegal entry as part of migrant caravan. Retrieved March 04, 2019, from https://www.usatoday.com/story/news/2018/11/30/dhs-murderer-gang-member-arrested-part-migrant-caravan/2163762002/

Kelly, G. (11 de enero de 2017). ¿Puedes distinguir los tweets reales de Donald Trump de las falsificaciones de MSM? Toma nuestro test para averiguarlo. Recuperado de https://www.telegraph.co.uk/men/the-filter/can-tell-real-donald-trump-tweets-msm-fakes-take-quiz-find/

Knobel, M. (1994). Adolescent Psychiatry Today. Past, Present and Future of Psychiatry. doi: 10.1142/9789814440912_0155

Le poivoir psychiatrique. (1973-1974). Cours Au College De Françe. Retrieved from www.fce.com.ar. ISBN 2-02-030769-3 Translaed in Spain by Horacio Ponce ISBN 978-950-557-637-1

Lotha, G., Sampaolo, M., Techs, N., & Zeidan, A. (2014, October 1). Islamic State in Iraq and the Levant | History & Facts. Retrieved September 26, 2019, from https://www.britannica.com/topic/Islamic-State-in-Iraq-and-the-Levant

Lotha, G., Sampaolo, M., Techs, N., & Zeidam, A. (2014b, October 1). Islamic State in Iraq and the Levant - Expansion and declaration of a caliphate. Retrieved September 26, 2019, from https://www.britannica.com/topic/Islamic-State-in-Iraq-and-the-Levant/Expansion-and-declaration-of-a-caliphate

Lotha, G., Rogers, K., & Sampaolo, M. (2019, June 23). Perceptual learning. Retrieved September 29, 2019, from https://www.britannica.com/topic/perceptual-learning

Macro-Theory: Definition of Macro-Theory by Lexico. (n.d.). Retrieved October 12, 2019, from https://www.lexico.com/en/definition/macro-theory.

Musacchio, & Aldo. (2012, July 13). Mexico's financial crisis of 1994-1995. Retrieved April 03, 2019, from https://dash.harvard.edu/handle/1/9056792

Nations, U. (2019a). Asylum. In U. S. America (Ed.), Standard Language Addendum: Asylum, Withholding of Removal & Convention Against Torture (p. 2). America: United States.

Nations, U. (2019b). Convention Against Torture. In U. S. America (Ed.), Standard Language Addendum: Asylum, Withholding of Removal. & Convention Against Torture (p. 9). America: United States.

N. R. (2010). Objetal Relationship and Development of Psiquism: A Psychoanalitic Conception. Universidad Nacional Mayor, Peru, 3, 221-230. Retrieved from talye_03@hotmail.com. UNMSM ISSN Print, 1560-909X. ISSN Electronic 1609-7475

Orr, G., Hesson, T., Choi, M., & Orr, G. (2019, January 09). From 'wall' to 'barrier': How Trump's vision for the border keeps changing. Retrieved May 13, 2019, from https://www.politico.com/story/2019/01/08/trumps-vision-wall-concrete-steel-changes-1088714

Papalia, D. I., Olds, S. W., & Feldman, R. D. (n.d.). Human Develop. Copyright by The McGraw-Hill Companies, Inc.

Sansal, P. (2019, June 18). Domesticating the Giant: The Global Governance of Migration. Retrieved September 29, 2019, from https://www.cfr.org/report/domesticating-giant-global-governance-migration

Smuggling of migrants: the harsh search for a better life. (n.d.). Retrieved September 25, 2019, from https://www.unodc.org/toc/en/crimes/migrant-smuggling.html

Swinford, S. (2011, May 5). Doubts grow on US version of strike against bin Laden. Retrieved September 29, 2019, from https://www.smh.com.au/world/doubts-grow-on-us-version-of-strike-against-bin-laden-20110505-1eaah.html

Swinford, S., & Souza, P. (2011, May 4). Osama bin Laden dead: Blackout during raid on bin Laden compound. Retrieved September 29, 2019, from https://www.telegraph.co.uk/news/worldnews/al-qaeda/8493391/Osama-bin-Laden-dead-Blackout-during-raid-on-bin-Laden-compound.html

Tanenhaus, S. (2018, October 11). How Trumpism Will Outlast Trump. Retrieved October 9, 2019, from https://time.com/magazine/us/5421567/october-22nd-2018-vol-192-no-16-u-s/.

The human dilemma: Rollo May. (1988). PsycEXTRA Dataset. doi:10.1037/e536832004-001

The Chatolic World. (2014/06/24/). How to Psychoanayze Yourself | Bishop Fulton J.Sheen. Retrivied From https://www.youtube.com/watch?v=k3rhPa7h4ro

The Chatolic World. (2014/06/24). Psychology and Psychiatry | Bishop Fulton J.Sheen. Retrivied from https://www.youtube.com/watch?v=L-5_RTREbUs

The Tequila crisis in 1994. (n.d.). Retrieved April 03, 2019, from https://economics.rabobank.com/publications/2013/september/the-tequila-crisis-in-1994/

Trotsenburg, A. V. (2019, March 29). Facing an Unprecedented Migration Crisis in Latin America and the Caribbean. Retrieved May 05, 2019, from https://www.worldbank.org/en/news/opinion/2019/03/29/america-latina-y-el-caribe-frente-a-una-crisis-migratoria-sin-precedentes.

Trump proposes solar panel wall for Mexican border. (2017, June 22). Retrieved May 13, 2019, from https://www.bbc.com/news/av/world-us-canada-40365031/trump-proposes-solar-panel-wall-for-mexican-border

Sociology Dictionary, O. E. (n.d.). macrosociology definition. Retrieved October 12, 2019, from https://sociologydictionary.org/macrosociology/.

UN, United Nations, UN Treaties, Treaties. (n.d.). Retrieved April 03, 2019, from https://treaties.un.org/pages/ViewDetails.aspx?src=TREATY&mtdsg_no=VI-15&chapter=6&clang=_en

Unodc.org. (2019). What is Human Trafficking?. [online] Available at: https://www.unodc.org/unodc/en/human-trafficking/what-is-human-trafficking.html [Accessed 23 Sep. 2019].

Unodc.org. (2019). UNODC Smuggling of Migrants. [online] Available at: https://www.unodc.org/unodc/en/human-trafficking/smuggling-of-migrants.html [Accessed 23 Sep. 2019].

U.S.-backed forces declare victory over ISIS in Syria. (2019, March 23). Retrieved April 05, 2019, from https://www.euronews.com/2019/03/23/u-s-backed-forces-declare-victory-over-isis-syria-n972401

Van Trotsenburg, A. (2019). Facing an Unprecedented Migration Crisis in Latin America and the Caribbean. [online] World Bank. Available at: https://www.worldbank.org/en/news/opinion/2019/03/29/america-latina-y-el-caribe-frente-a-una-crisis-migratoria-sin-precedentes [Accessed 23 Sep. 2019].

Wikipedia. (2019, September 24). conspiracy theories about when and how Osama bin Laden died. Retrieved September 29, 2019, from https://en.wikipedia.org/wiki/Osama_bin_Laden_death_conspiracy_theories

What is Human Trafficking? (n.d.). Retrieved September 25, 2019, from https://www.unodc.org/unodc/en/human-trafficking/what-is-human-trafficking.html

Worldwide Religious Persecution. (2018, November 6). Retrieved October 12, 2019, from https://www.nae.net/worldwide-religious-persecution/.

Zeidan, A., Lotha, G., Young, G., Techs, N., Cunningham, J. M., Sinha, S., & Sampaulo, M. (2011, July 6). Syrian Civil War | Facts & Timeline. Retrieved September 26, 2019, from https://www.britannica.com/event/Syrian-Civil-War

*Just how screen us in that book itself haven't political publishment. alone step a new vison over Mental health Ivesntment; a greatest path to Proffesional Healthness to thise reason **anyone more should set acces to its** Because itself are what them need to make a better awere about their proffesional area, appontishment than **this might not be selled or readed to anyone wich has not allowed by an Academic Institutions In Psychoanalizes or Rewardless Mental Health** giving a Student Card or in other manner His Proffesional ID Card.*

www.ingramcontent.com/pod-product-compliance
Lightning Source LLC
Chambersburg PA
CBHW070745250726
48662CB00004B/1646